Simply Excel

Ramon Zamora
Bob Albrecht

Osborne **McGraw-Hill**

Berkeley New York St. Louis San Francisco
Auckland Bogotá Hamburg London Madrid
Mexico City Milan Montreal New Delhi Panama City
Paris São Paulo Singapore
Sydney Tokyo Toronto

Osborne **McGraw-Hill**
2600 Tenth Street
Berkeley, California 94710
U.S.A.

For information on software, translations, or book distributors outside of the U.S.A., please write to Osborne **McGraw-Hill** at the above address.

Simply Excel

Copyright © 1993 by McGraw-Hill, Inc. All rights reserved. Printed in the United States of America. Except as permitted under the Copyright Act of 1976, no part of this publication may be reproduced or distributed in any form or by any means, or stored in a database or retrieval system, without the prior written permission of the publisher, with the exception that the program listings may be entered, stored, and executed in a computer system, but they may not be reproduced for publication.

1234567890 DOC 99876543

ISBN 0-07-881883-4

Information has been obtained by Osborne **McGraw-Hill** from sources believed to be reliable. However, because of the possibility of human or mechanical error by our sources, Osborne **McGraw-Hill**, or others, Osborne **McGraw-Hill** does not guarantee the accuracy, adequacy, or completeness of any information and is not responsible for any errors or omissions or the results obtained from use of such information.

Acknowledgments

The Authors extend a special "thank you" to the following people:

All of the "turned on to learning" students in The Science School at Piner High School, Santa Rosa, CA, who tested the draft versions of this book, and provided many helpful comments and inventive suggestions.

Each of the resourceful and dedicated people at Osborne McGraw-Hill who pooled their talents to make a book like this one actually happen.

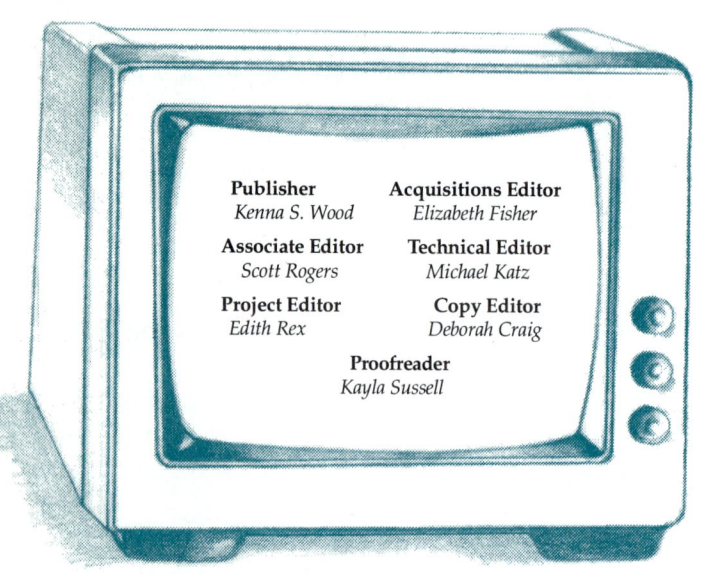

Publisher
Kenna S. Wood

Acquisitions Editor
Elizabeth Fisher

Associate Editor
Scott Rogers

Technical Editor
Michael Katz

Project Editor
Edith Rex

Copy Editor
Deborah Craig

Proofreader
Kayla Sussell

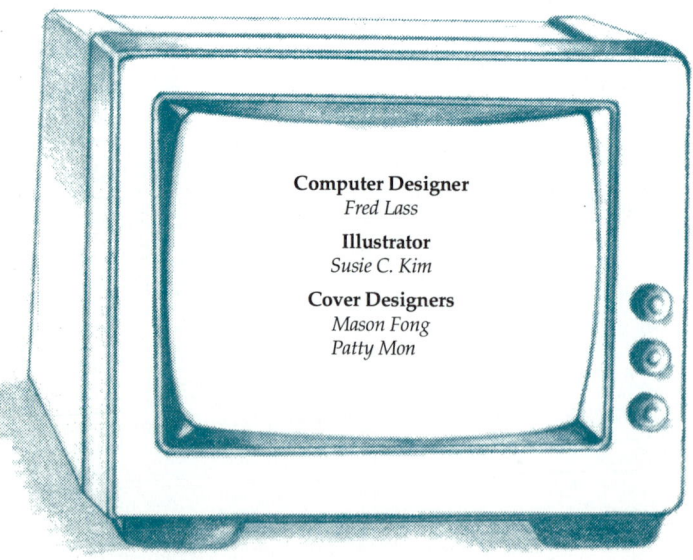

Computer Designer
Fred Lass

Illustrator
Susie C. Kim

Cover Designers
Mason Fong
Patty Mon

Contents

1 **Introduction to Excel**
   1

2 **Worksheet Explorations**
   17

3 **Excel Charts**
   41

4 **Excel Databases**
   57

5 **Worksheet Magic**
   79

6 **Chart Power**
   101

7 **Workbooks and Links**
   129

8 **Notes and Other Features**
   155

A	*Installing Excel on Your Computer*	*165*
B	*Toolbars: Check Access to Tools*	*169*
C	*The Excel 4.0 Environment*	*177*
D	*Function Junction*	*183*
E	*Reading About Excel*	*195*
	Index	*197*

It's Simple to Use This Lay-Flat Binding ...

Open this book to any page you choose and crease back the left-hand page by pressing along the length of the spine with your fingers. Now, the book will stay open until you're ready to go on to another page.

Unlike regular book bindings, this special binding won't weaken or crack when you crease back the pages. It's tough, durable, and resilient—designed to withstand years of daily use. So go ahead, put this book to the test and use it as often as you like.

Introduction to Excel

1

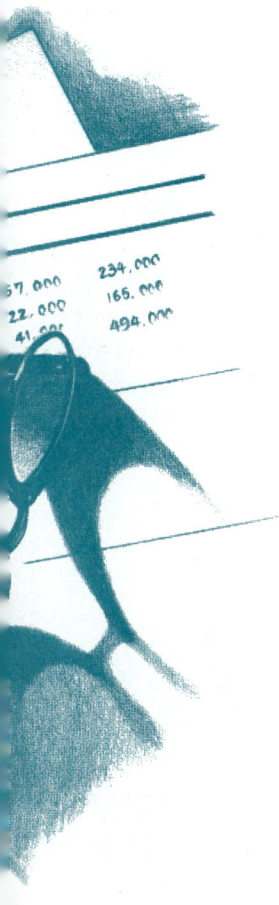

This book introduces you to Microsoft Excel, a powerful software package designed to help you with both simple and complex calculations. Excel is one of several popular *spreadsheet* programs—programs specifically created to perform electronic number crunching and data organization tasks. Excel provides an integrated set of the latest calculation tools, including graphics and presentation features that let you generate professional-looking reports. Excel runs on IBM PC (or compatible) computers that use Microsoft Windows, and also on Apple Macintosh systems.

What Is a Spreadsheet Program?

An electronic spreadsheet, the modern equivalent of three familiar bookkeeping tools (paper ledger sheets, pencils, and calculators), puts enormous computational power under your control. Lengthy calculations that you normally do by hand can be done on the computer in seconds or minutes. You can chart and graph data like a skilled artist with the push of a button.

Traditional bookkeeping tools

How is all this possible? Excel employs a common data structure for its stored information. This common data structure enables you to manipulate data and graphics with ease. For example, Excel lets you create a list of data using its database tools, transfer the list to a worksheet area for calculations, chart the results of the calculations, and print a finished report using its presentation tools and printer options. When you use an integrated software package like Excel, you seldom have to reenter data for another part of the worksheet or program. The common data structure and the program's copy and paste tools let you move data automatically.

Modern spreadsheet user

Key Excel Tools and Features

Excel's three primary spreadsheet tools are the worksheet, the database, and charts. *Worksheets* are Excel's electronic versions of paper ledger sheets. Worksheet documents display data, text, and graphics in neat rows and columns. You can alter worksheets and worksheet data easily, and display information in a variety of formats and styles. Worksheets and Excel's worksheet tools form the backbone of the Excel spreadsheet package.

4   Simply Excel

	A	B	C	D	E	F	G
5	**Initial Data**						
6	LOAN DATA				TABLE DATA		
7		Loan amount:	$20,000.00		Table starts at date:		
8		Annual interest rate:	11.00%		or at payment number:	1	
9		Term in years:	4				
10		Payments per year:	12				
11		First payment due:	9/14/93				
12	PERIODIC PAYMENT						
13		Entered payment:			The table uses the calculated periodic payment amount		
14		Calculated payment:	$516.91		unless you enter a value for "Entered payment".		
15	CALCULATIONS						
16		Use payment of:	$516.91		Beginning balance at payment 1:		20,000.00
17		1st payment in table:	1		Cumulative interest prior to payment 1:		0.00
18	**Table**						
19							
20		Payment	Beginning			Ending	Cumulative
21	No.	Date	Balance	Interest	Principal	Balance	Interest
22	1	9/14/93	20,000.00	183.33	333.58	19,666.42	183.33
23	2	10/14/93	19,666.42	180.28	336.63	19,329.79	363.61
24	3	11/14/93	19,329.79	177.19	339.72	18,990.07	540.80
25	4	12/14/93	18,990.07	174.08	342.83	18,647.23	714.87
26	5	1/14/94	18,647.23	170.93	345.98	18,301.25	885.81

Example Excel worksheet

With Excel, you can organize a set of worksheet data into a systematic arrangement of related information called a *database*. One example of a typical database is a telephone directory, which includes names, addresses, and telephone numbers. After you organize worksheet entries into a database, Excel lets you use standard database operations to search, sort, and retrieve database elements.

	A	B	C	D	E	F	G
1							
2							
3		Date	Salesperson	Customer	Product	Quan	Total Sale
4		6/4	H. Carlson	Centers, Inc.	Lumber	175	2,100
5		6/5	E. Simpson	Homes Corp.	Lumber	255	3,060
6		6/5	L. Diaz	Future Grids	Nails	135	74
7		6/6	H. Carlson	Brilanica & Beam	Bricks	655	590
8		6/6	L. Diaz	Quick Repair Co.	Nails	355	195
9		6/11	L. Diaz	Homes Corp.	Bricks	175	158
10		6/12	H. Carlson	Centers, Inc.	Lumber	265	3,180
11		6/13	E. Simpson	Homes Corp.	Lumber	355	4,260
12		6/14	L. Diaz	Future Grids	Nails	140	77
13		6/15	H. Carlson	Brilanica & Beam	Bricks	165	149
14		6/16	L. Diaz	Quick Repair Co.	Nails	175	96
15		6/17	L. Diaz	Homes Corp.	Bricks	165	149
16		6/18	H. Carlson	Centers, Inc.	Lumber	265	3,180
17		6/19	E. Simpson	Homes Corp.	Lumber	226	2,712
18		6/20	L. Diaz	Future Grids	Nails	126	69
19		6/21	H. Carlson	Brilanica & Beam	Bricks	176	158
20		6/22	L. Diaz	Quick Repair Co.	Nails	105	58
21		6/23	L. Diaz	Homes Corp.	Bricks	175	158
22		6/24	H. Carlson	Centers, Inc.	Lumber	150	1,800
23		6/25	E. Simpson	Homes Corp.	Lumber	175	2,100
24		6/26	L. Diaz	Future Grids	Nails	126	69
25		6/27	H. Carlson	Brilanica & Beam	Bricks	185	167

Example Excel database

Excel's *chart* tools let you transform worksheet data into graphs. Excel supports 14 chart types including both two- and three-dimensional graphs. You can display each chart type in a variety of formats.

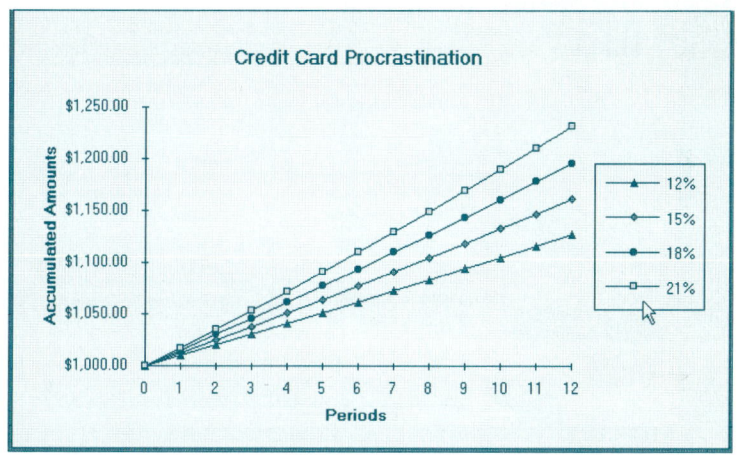

Example Excel chart

In addition to these three primary spreadsheet tools—the worksheet, the database, and charts—Excel provides *presentation* tools that help you control the format and design of your printed reports. Presentation tools include features that let you perform specific worksheet tasks such as controlling how information looks, drawing objects, and formatting tables.

Excel has a *macro* feature for automating repetitive tasks and customizing Excel itself. Macros are stored sequences of keystrokes and menu selections that Excel "plays back" to perform a set of tasks automatically. You build Excel macros by using the program's record and playback features.

The Excel package also includes a set of on-line tools to help you learn how to use the program. Excel's learning tools include interesting, animated tutorials that demonstrate how to use the program and its many features. Excel's comprehensive on-line help feature provides detailed reference information about Excel and its operations.

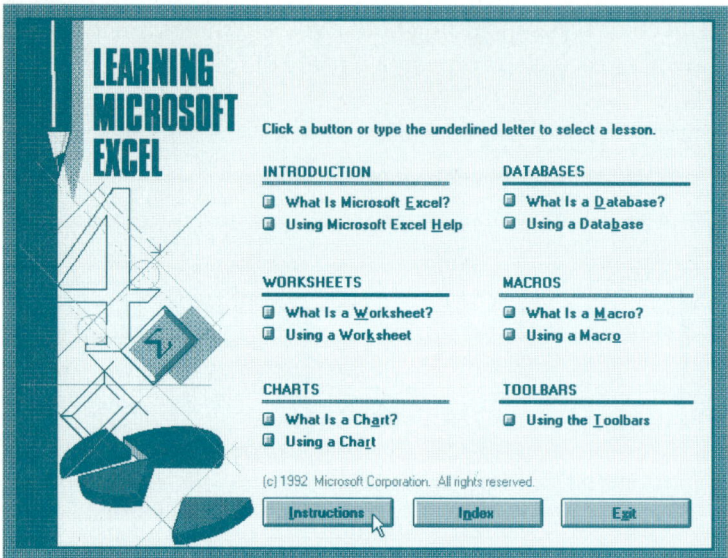

Excel tutorial screen

Who Uses Spreadsheets?

Most people who use integrated spreadsheet packages do so in their work activities. Spreadsheet programs such as Excel have become essential workplace productivity tools. They are used to calculate budgets, make forecasts, manage operations, do financial analyses, prepare financial statements and presentations, and maintain and update all types of numerical data.

Spreadsheets, which were once used mainly by large corporations and professional analysts, are now being employed in small businesses. Print shops use spreadsheets to help generate bids, keep track of inventories, and monitor job loads. Small cafe owners use databases and spreadsheets to track the type of meals, drinks, and desserts being purchased. Bakeries use spreadsheets to set finished product prices based on calculated production costs. Of the over 30 million people who work at home in the U.S., many routinely use spreadsheet programs.

Typical spreadsheet users

Students are also learning to use spreadsheets to solve homework problems and to graph results. With programs like Excel, you can develop automated spreadsheets for use by people who know almost nothing about computers. For example, a teacher might prepare a science experiment calculation as an automated worksheet. The worksheet could prompt students for laboratory data, verify input values, and plot experimental results. The students supplying input values would not have to know in detail how spreadsheets work.

In this book, you will encounter interesting and unique spreadsheet applications. These applications demonstrate how Excel's tools and features help you crunch numbers and display results. They also provide you with practical examples of how you might use spreadsheets, in business, at school, and in the home.

Introducing...Excel!

A blank or empty worksheet, the primary Excel tool, appears when you start the program. If you need specific instructions on how to install and start Excel on your computer, refer to Appendix A.

Four horizontal bars extend across the top of the blank worksheet. You see a *title bar*, a *menu bar*, a *toolbar*, and a *formula bar*. Across the bottom of the window is a *status bar*.

8 Simply Excel

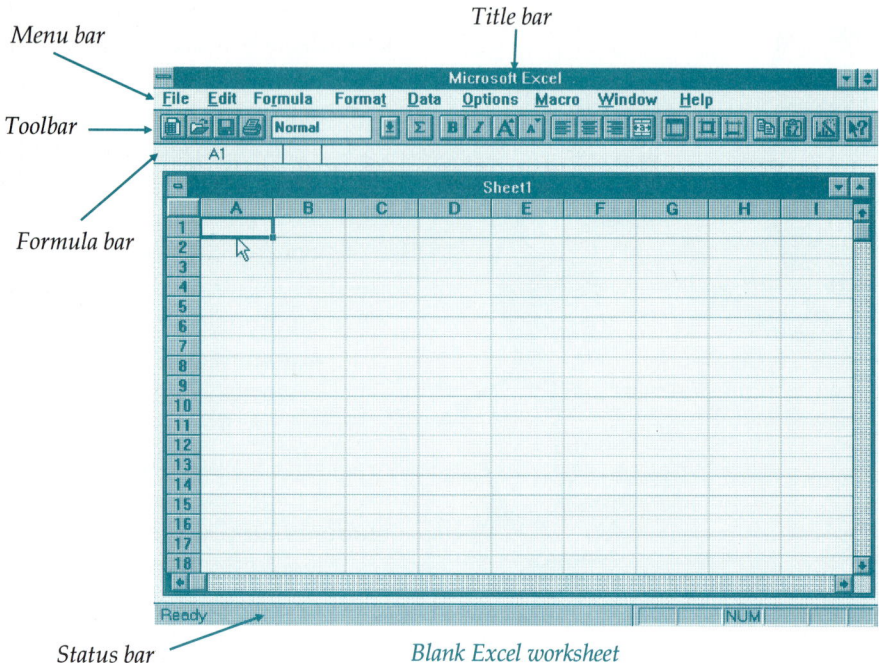

Blank Excel worksheet

The menu bar and toolbar let you control Excel's features and operations as you build a worksheet application. The menu bar gives you access to Excel's commands. The items on this bar change with the type of Excel document being displayed. For example, when you are working with a chart document, the menu bar displays menus of chart commands.

The toolbar consists of a collection of *icons,* or graphic symbols, arranged horizontally across the screen. You can use the toolbar to quickly perform certain tasks that would otherwise involve selecting several menu bar commands. The toolbar has been designed to handle many of the more common worksheet tasks such as adding graphic elements and altering the format of worksheet data. You can also move the toolbar to different locations on the screen, and can customize it to meet your needs. Excel has other specialized toolbars that you can display and reposition on the screen.

For more information about Excel's toolbars, refer to Appendix B, "Toolbars: Click Access to Tools."

Chapter 1: Introduction to Excel

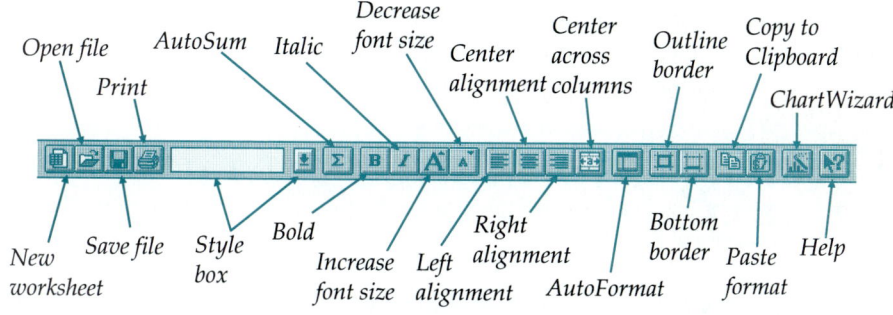

Standard toolbar

Each intersection of a row and column on a worksheet is called a *cell*. An Excel worksheet is like an extremely large piece of paper that is divided into 256 *columns* (vertical divisions on the page) and 16,384 *rows* (horizontal divisions on the page). On the empty worksheet, you see eighteen rows numbered 1 to 18, and nine columns labeled A to I.

Given this total number of rows and columns, an Excel worksheet potentially has room for over 4 million cells. In practice, however, few spreadsheet applications ever require even close to that many cell locations.

When you move the mouse pointer to a cell and click, a highlight or border appears around that cell.

A worksheet is like a big sheet of paper

The highlighted cell becomes the *active cell* on the worksheet. The formula bar provides you with information about the active cell. You use special areas on the formula bar to edit the contents of the active cell.

The status bar at the bottom of the screen displays status and summary information related to the current Excel command.

Entering Information into a Worksheet

Worksheet cells hold two types of information: constant values and formulas. *Constant values* are data items that you enter directly into a cell location. These values can be either numeric (numbers, dates, or times) or text (labels and notes).

Formulas are equations that you want Excel to evaluate. When Excel encounters a formula, it calculates a numerical result for the formula, displaying the result in that formula's cell location.

Let's explore how a simple worksheet is developed. If possible, try to replicate the worksheet on your own computer. Because of size limitations, this book does not attempt to provide detailed, step-by-step tutorial instructions for worksheet examples. However, the discussion of each example includes enough information (data, formulas, and screen images) to create an actual worksheet.

Suppose you wish to calculate the total cost of an item whose sales price is $1,000. Unless you live in Oregon, the total cost will be the sales price plus an assessment for your local sales tax. Suppose your local sales tax rate is 8 percent.

A simple worksheet to perform this calculation might have the constant text values (labels) "Price," "Tax (%)," and "Total" in cells A1, A2, and A3, respectively.

Note: If you enter these labels, you do not enter the quotation marks or the commas.

Chapter 1: Introduction to Excel   **11**

Worksheet with labels

The constant numeric value 1000, the item's price, goes in cell B1. The tax rate, 8, goes in cell B2.

Constant numeric values in place

Cell B3 will contain the calculated total cost. A formula to calculate the total cost will be attached to cell B3.

Formulas in Excel always start with an equal sign (=). A formula can include constants, references to other cells, arithmetic symbols, and the names of Excel functions that perform specific types of calculations.

For this example, the formula for the total cost might look like this:

=B1 * (1 + B2 / 100)

Cell B1 contains the price of the item. Cell B2 contains the tax rate. The formula tells Excel to take the contents of cell B2, divide it by 100 (to change it into a decimal fraction), add the fraction to 1, and multiply that result by the contents of cell B2 (Price). This formula is shorthand for:

Total = Price * (1 + Tax(%) / 100)

Formula in place

When you attach the formula for the total cost to cell B3, Excel instantly calculates the result, 1080, and displays that value in cell B3. The formula attached to cell B3 appears in the formula bar.

When Excel encounters the formula at cell B3, it replaces the cell references (B1, B2) in the equation with the constant values (1000 and 8) and calculates the total cost. Here are possible interim results that Excel might produce as it evaluates the formula at cell B3:

=B1 * (1 + B2 / 100)
=1000 * (1 + 8 / 100)
=1000 * (1 + .08)
=1000 * 1.08
=1080

The key advantages of using an electronic worksheet rather than pencil and paper is that a spreadsheet enables you to do the following:

- Change selected data items quickly and easily
- Calculate new results instantly
- Eliminate calculation errors

For example, suppose the price of the item you wish to purchase is $2,000 instead of $1,000. No problem for an electronic worksheet! You simply change the value in cell B1, and a new total cost instantly appears in cell B3.

	A	B	C	D	E	F	G	H
1	Price	2000						
2	Tax (%)	8						
3	Total	2160						
4								
5								
6								
7								
8								
9								
10								
11								
12								
13								
14								
15								
16								
17								

New cost total based on new price

When you use a worksheet formula (like the one in cell B3), changing any constant value referenced by the formula generates a new result. Suppose the tax rate in your area is only 5 percent. Changing the value in cell B2 to 5 produces a new total cost, 2100, for the higher priced item.

New total cost based on lower tax rate

A worksheet's ability to instantly evaluate "what if" questions such as "What if the price is double?" or "What if the tax rate is 5 percent instead of 8 percent?" demonstrates why spreadsheet programs have become so popular. You no longer spend time repeating messy calculations and generating hard-to-find errors. You simply change constant values on the worksheet. The program quickly recalculates formulas and displays new results based on the changes you made.

This concludes your introduction to the Microsoft Excel integrated spreadsheet package. The following chapters explore in greater detail the use of Excel's worksheet, database, and chart tools. In these chapters, you will find example applications that fully illustrate how you might use Excel's foremost features and capabilities.

Worksheet Explorations

18 Simply Excel

In this chapter, you examine two interesting Excel worksheet applications. You explore worksheets that help you analyze utility bills and perform credit card interest computations. To start, take a moment to review the similarity of the Excel worksheet environments on Apple Macintosh and PC computers.

Using Excel on Different Computers

Excel is available for both Apple Macintosh and PC (or compatible) computers. The Excel programs look nearly identical and operate similarly on the two computers.

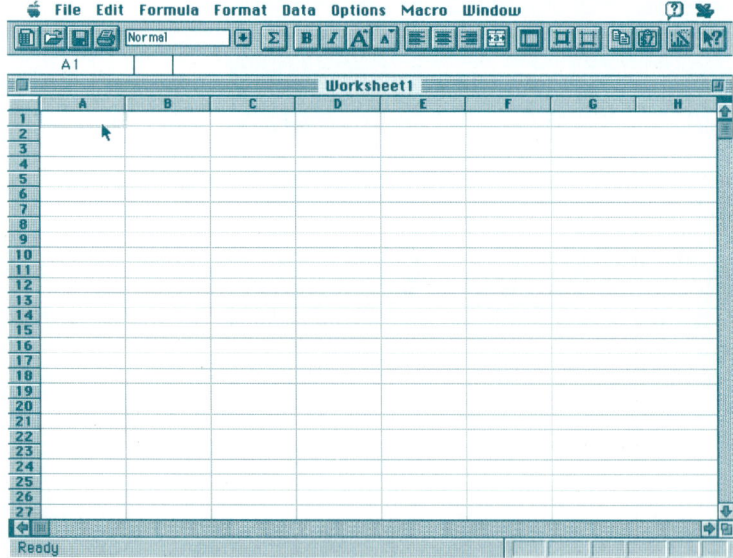

Excel on a Macintosh

When you compare the Excel Macintosh and PC screens, you see a few cosmetic differences. The Macintosh menu bar shows an "apple" icon on the

Chapter 2: Worksheet Explorations 19

left side and does not include the Help option. On a Macintosh, you access Help either from Excel's Window menu or from the system Help menu. If you are running Excel on the Macintosh under System 7.0 or under Multi-Finder, you will see a Help icon on the right side of the menu bar as well. The icon looks like a cartoon bubble with a question mark (?) in it.

The PC menu bar has no apple icon, does show a Help option, and underlines the letters you use when activating menus from the keyboard. For example, the letter "F" in File is underlined.

Excel on a PC

Menu commands and product features on both versions were designed to be identical. Any operation you perform on the Macintosh can be duplicated on the PC, and vice versa. If you are using Excel with a pointing device such as a mouse, there is almost no variance in the way the products work.

Because of Excel's compatibility across computer platforms, this book shows example screen images for the PC version only. If you are using Excel on a Macintosh, you will have no problem correlating this book's images with your Excel screens.

A Worksheet for Utility Bills

Almost every home and business gets a utility bill each month. Typical utility bills itemize how much gas, electricity, and water have been used, and how much money is owed to the utility company. Some bills include surcharges for sewer usage and for refuse pickup.

In the following example, you learn how to use an Excel worksheet to check a simplified utility bill from the People's Energy Company. For this example, the worksheet has been designed to

People's Energy Company						
	Period:		Quantity:			
Type of Service:	from	to	therms	kwh		Amount
GAS	8/24/93	9/24/93	53.8		$	28.27
ELEC				698.7		77.60
			TOTAL CURRENT CHARGES			105.87
			PREVIOUS BALANCE			123.45
			PAYMENT: 9/7/93			-123.45
			TOTAL AMOUNT NOW DUE		$	105.87
GAS RATE:	0.52538 per therm					
ELEC RATE:	0.11107 per kwh					

People's Energy Company worksheet

look somewhat like an actual bill. Excel gives you tremendous control over both worksheet calculations and the way a finished worksheet looks and gets printed.

The worksheet indicates the amount of energy used for two types of services: gas and electricity. The quantity of gas used is recorded in therms. The quantity of electrical energy is recorded in kilowatt-hours.

The billing amounts on the worksheet are calculated by multiplying the quantities of energy by the rates. The rate for gas is $0.52538 per therm. The electricity rate is $0.11107 per kilowatt-hour (kwh).

Worksheet Labels First

You can begin developing a worksheet in a variety of ways. One approach involves putting all of the worksheet's labels in place first. Entering the labels helps you locate the remaining cells that will hold data and formulas.

Note: Most of this book's illustrations, like the one that follows, are cropped to show only part of the worksheet screen. The images on your computer will always show the complete worksheet display.

Chapter 2: Worksheet Explorations

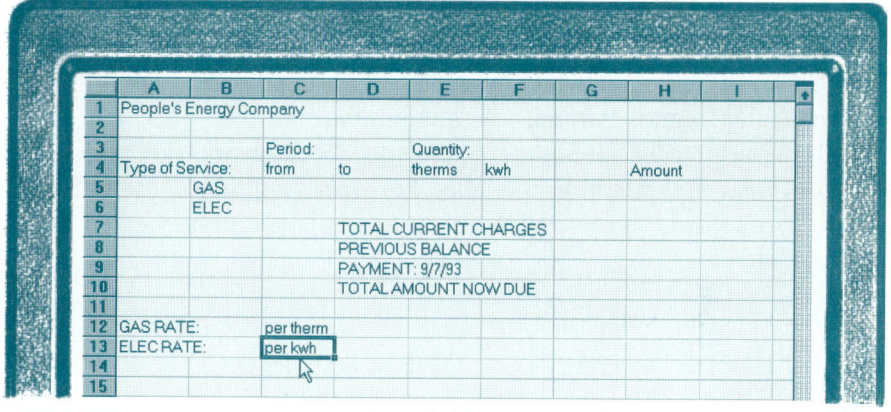

Worksheet labels in place

The labels for the People's Energy Company worksheet appear in the following cells:

Cell   Label Text
A1   People's Energy Company
C3   Period:
E3   Quantity:
A4   A4 Type of Service:
C4   from
D4   to
E4   therms
F4   kwh
H4   Amount
B5   GAS
B6   ELEC
D7   TOTAL CURRENT CHARGES
D8   PREVIOUS BALANCE
D9   PAYMENT: 9/7/93
D10   TOTAL AMOUNT NOW DUE
A12   GAS RATE:
C12   per therm
A13   ELEC RATE:
C13   per kwh

Some of these labels fit into a single cell. The rest, such as "People's Energy Company," are wider than the default column width of the cell holding the label. In Excel, when you enter a wide label into a narrow cell, the label automatically extends into the adjacent empty cells.

If the adjacent cells are not empty, a wide label appears truncated to the width of the cell containing the label. For truncated labels, the full label text remains stored in the computer's memory, and can be viewed in the formula bar.

Worksheet Numeric Constants Next

Once the worksheet labels are in place, you can enter any numeric constants. For this example, you can enter the data for periods (from, to), quantities (therms, kwh), previous balance, payment, and rates.

	A	B	C	D	E	F	G	H	I
1	People's Energy Company								
2									
3			Period:		Quantity:				
4	Type of Service:		from	to	therms	kwh		Amount	
5		GAS	8/24/93	9/24/93	53.8				
6		ELEC				698.7			
7				TOTAL CURRENT CHARGES					
8				PREVIOUS BALANCE				123.45	
9				PAYMENT: 9/7/93				-123.45	
10				TOTAL AMOUNT NOW DUE					
11									
12	GAS RATE	0.52538	per therm						
13	ELEC RATE	0.11107	per kwh						
14									
15									
16									

Numeric constants in place

The numeric constants for this worksheet include two dates and six numbers. Excel understands several different types of numeric constants including plain numbers, dates, and times. Here are the values, cell locations, and implied units for this worksheet's numeric constants. The units are for reference only; you do not have to enter them into the worksheet.

Cell	Value	Units
C5	8/24/93	Date
D5	9/24/93	Date
E5	53.8	therms
F6	698.7	kwh
H8	123.45	$ (Previous Balance)
H9	-123.45	$ (Payment: 9/7/93)
B12	0.52538	$/therm
B13	0.11107	$/kwh

When you enter the rate values in cells B12 and B13, notice that the two rate labels (GAS RATE: and ELEC RATE:) now appear truncated in cells A12 and A13, respectively. Since cells B12 and B13 are no longer empty, the labels in cells A12 and A13 cannot automatically extend to their full widths. You can remedy this problem later when you format and style the worksheet.

Adding Worksheet Formulas

The next step in building the worksheet involves adding formulas to specific cells. As you enter each formula into the formula bar, a result appears on the worksheet at the formula's cell location. When all the formulas are in place, you have a rough version of the completed worksheet.

Formulas in place

All the formulas for this worksheet go into cells in column H, the Amount column. The formulas for calculating the amount owed for gas and electricity, the total of these two amounts, and the total bill are included here. The "Formula Computes" information indicates the purpose of the calculation.

Cell	Formula	Formula Computes
H5	=E5*B12	GAS Amount
H6	=F6*B13	ELEC Amount
H7	=H5+H6	TOTAL CURRENT CHARGES
H10	=H7+H8+H9	TOTAL AMOUNT NOW DUE

In cell H5, multiplying the number of therms used (E5) times the GAS RATE (B12) yields the billing amount for gas, which is 28.26544. In Excel, the formula for this calculation looks like this: =E5*B12. Remember, Excel formulas always start with an equal sign (=).

The calculation for the electricity billing amount multiplies the number of kilowatt-hours (F6) times the ELEC RATE (B13). When you enter that formula (=F6*B13) into cell H6, the result of that computation (77.60461) appears at that location. After you have entered a formula, you can click the cell that contains it to view and edit the formula in the formula bar.

The last two formulas in the Amount column (in cells H7 and H10) calculate the TOTAL CURRENT CHARGES and TOTAL AMOUNT NOW DUE, respectively.

At this point, the worksheet is usable but not well organized visually. The labels for GAS RATE and ELEC RATE remain truncated. The numbers in the Amount column are not uniform; some show too many decimal places. The Period and Quantity constants are not aligned well under their column labels. Using Excel, you can easily format this worksheet into a professional-looking document

Formatting Your Worksheet

Excel lets you control every element of a cell, including the font (typeface), the font style (plain, bold, italic), and the point size. You can also control the alignment of information within a cell and the formatting of data (number of decimal positions, use of commas and dollar signs, and how negative numbers are displayed).

Chapter 2: Worksheet Explorations

You control most of these options by first selecting a cell or range of cells, and then using menu commands or toolbar icons to initiate the changes. For example, suppose you wish to boldface and increase the point size of the worksheet label "People's Energy Company." First, you click cell A1 to select that cell and its contents, a label.

Cell A1 selected

When the cell is selected, you choose the Font command on the Format menu. This brings up a Font dialog box from which you can select the typeface (Font), the font style, and the point size. In the example, the initial font is "Helv," which stands for the Helvetica font. Based on how you installed Excel, your dialog box may show a different initial font selection.

If you want to change the text in cell A1 to size 12 bold, select those size and style options from the appropriate list boxes. The Sample window in the bottom half of the dialog box shows what the text will look like with the new settings.

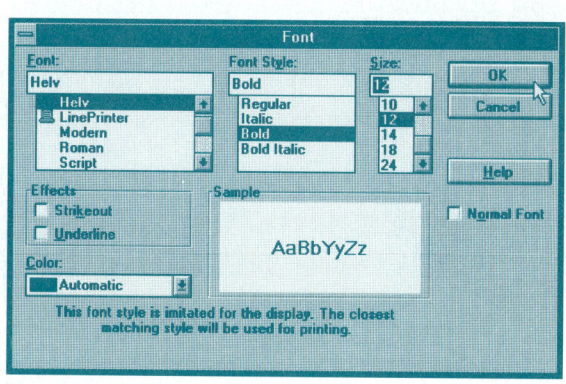

Font dialog box

26 Simply Excel

Once the sample text looks the way you want, clicking the OK button applies the settings to the selected cell, A1. If you select a range of cells, you can apply font, style, and size changes to all of those cells at once.

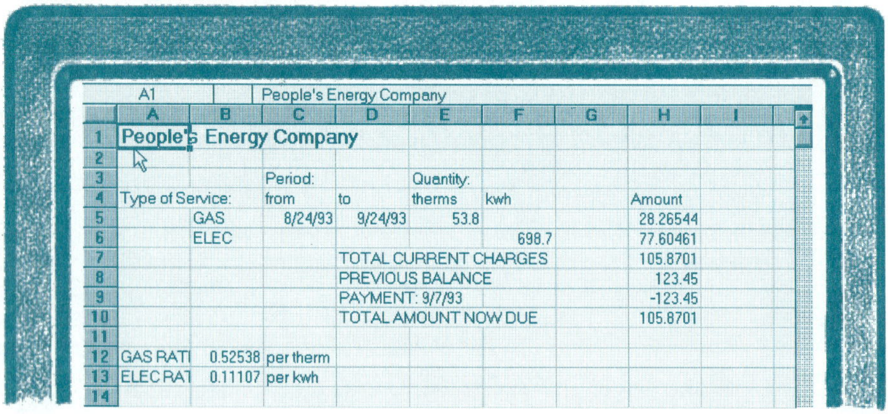

Reformatted contents of cell A1

To change the point size of a range of cells, first select all the cells to be reformatted. Suppose you wanted to reduce the contents of text in cells A3 through H13. Click and drag from cell A3 to cell H13 to select this range of cells. A highlight will cover the selected cells.

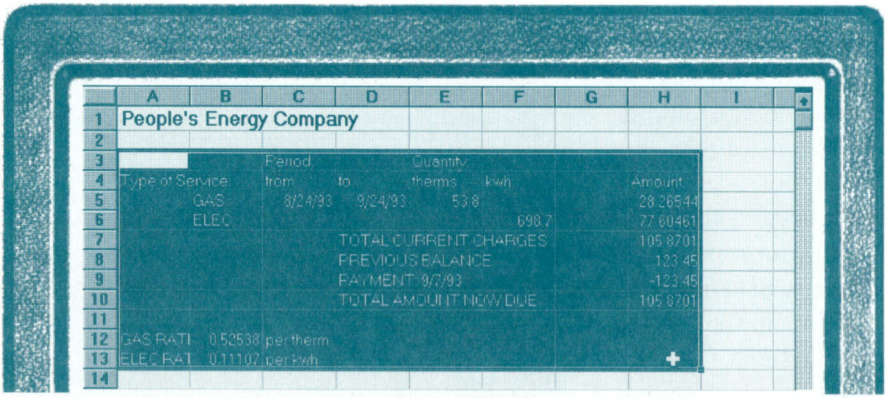

Range of cells selected

Chose the Font command on the Format menu to again display the Font dialog box. The initial point size is 10. If you select 8 from the Size list, check the Sample window to see how the text will appear on the screen.

Chapter 2: Worksheet Explorations   27

Once you select a new point size for the range of cells, clicking the OK button applies the setting you have selected. The information in cells A3 through H13 appears in the smaller point size. Note that this modification allows the labels in cells A12 and A13 to show completely.

Reformatted cell range

You can change certain font attributes by using the toolbar icons. For example, suppose you want to boldface all the labels on rows 3 and 4 of the worksheet. First, select those two rows of information. A highlight defines the selected region.

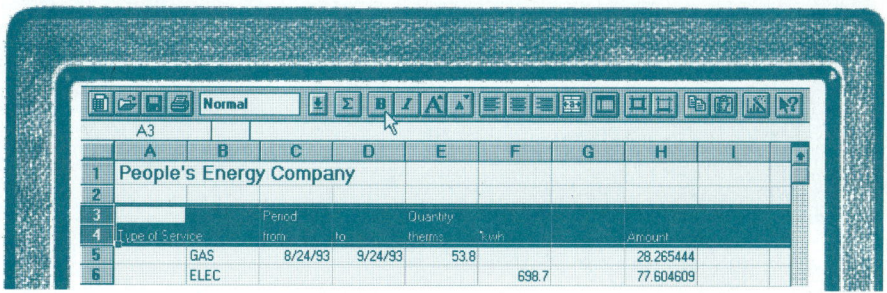

Rows of labels selected

The toolbar includes a Bold icon (marked with the letter B). If you click this icon, the information in the selected cells becomes bold. Such toolbar icons are shortcuts to using Excel menu commands. To boldface text using the menu bar, you have to open the Format menu, chose the Font command, select Bold in the Font Style list, and then click OK. You can accomplish the same thing with a single click on the toolbar's Bold icon.

Reformatted labels

The numeric constants in the Period and Quantity columns are aligned to the right side of the cells. The labels in these columns are aligned to the left side. Excel automatically right justifies numeric constants and left justifies text.

The two different alignments make it difficult to read the information. You can change the alignment of a range of cells by selecting the cells and clicking one of the three alignment icons on the toolbar. In this case you would select cells C5 through F6.

Range of numeric constants selected

If you select a range of cells and click the Left Alignment icon on the toolbar, Excel shifts the contents of the selected cells to the left. This slight change helps make the worksheet data more readable.

Chapter 2: Worksheet Explorations

Realigned group of constants

You need to make one final formatting adjustment to clean up the results in the Amount column. The data in this column represent dollars and cents. These values

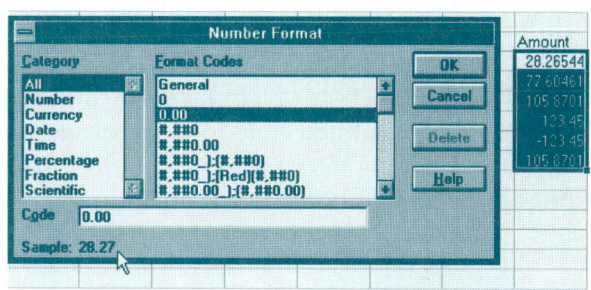

Number Format dialog box

require just two digits after the decimal point. If you select the cells containing numbers (cells H5 through H10), open the Format menu, and chose the Number command, you see the Number Format dialog box.

The Category list box on the left side of the dialog box shows the types of data you can restrict your formatting choices to: numbers, currency, dates, times, percentages, and so forth. The Format Codes list box displays the formatting options available for the type of data selected in the Category list box. If you select the 0.00 code, the sample at the bottom of the box indicates how the cell contents will be formatted. In this case, the value in cell H5 will be rounded up from 28.26544 to 28.27. If you click OK, Excel applies the selected format settings to the highlighted range of cells in column H.

At this point, the People's Energy Company worksheet is both functional (it works!) and readable. Excel provides additional format commands that let you add interesting professional touches to an operational worksheet.

Reformatted amount values

	A	B	C	D	E	F	G	H	I
1	People's Energy Company								
2									
3			Period:		Quantity:				
4	Type of Service:		from	to	therms	kwh		Amount	
5		GAS	8/24/93	9/24/93	53.8		$	28.27	
6		ELEC				698.7		77.60	
7					TOTAL CURRENT CHARGES			105.87	
8					PREVIOUS BALANCE			123.45	
9					PAYMENT: 9/7/93			-123.45	
10					TOTAL AMOUNT NOW DUE		$	105.87	
11									
12	GAS RATE:		0.52538	per therm					
13	ELEC RATE:		0.11107	per kwh					
14									
15									

People's Energy Company worksheet

The Patterns and Border commands on the Format menu have been used to add shaded or colored areas to the worksheet and place borders around selected cell ranges. If you wish to do this, experiment on your own. Try adding patterns and borders to worksheet regions.

Save the Worksheet

If you have been creating the example utility bill worksheet on your computer, this would be a good time to save your worksheet. To save a worksheet, choose the Save command from the File menu. A Save As dialog box will appear. You can then name the worksheet file and save it to disk. For more information about naming, saving, and using Excel files, refer to Appendix C, "The Excel 4.1 Environment."

Credit Card Procrastination Worksheet

Today, millions of people of all ages carry and use credit cards. Some people pay off their credit card balances each month. Others pay only part of the balances and accumulate interest charges on the unpaid amounts. A

Chapter 2: Worksheet Explorations

few people procrastinate, make late or infrequent payments, and accrue large interest penalties.

Although it's unlikely, what if someone charged $1,000 on a credit card and didn't make a payment for one year? How much interest would it cost that person? How much interest would accrue at different interest rates?

You can easily solve this hypothetical problem with an Excel worksheet.

	A	B	C	D	E
1	The Cost of Credit Card Procrastination				
2					
3	Annual interest rate (%)	12%	15%	18%	21%
4	Monthly interest rate	0.01	0.0125	0.015	0.0175
5	Monthly multiplier	1.01000	1.01250	1.01500	1.01750
6	Original amount ($)	$1,000	$1,000	$1,000	$1,000
7	After 1 month	$1,010	$1,013	$1,015	$1,018
8	After 2 months	$1,020	$1,025	$1,030	$1,035
9	After 3 months	$1,030	$1,038	$1,046	$1,053
10	After 4 months	$1,041	$1,051	$1,061	$1,072
11	After 5 months	$1,051	$1,064	$1,077	$1,091
12	After 6 months	$1,062	$1,077	$1,093	$1,110
13	After 7 months	$1,072	$1,091	$1,110	$1,129
14	After 8 months	$1,083	$1,104	$1,126	$1,149
15	After 9 months	$1,094	$1,118	$1,143	$1,169
16	After 10 months	$1,105	$1,132	$1,161	$1,189
17	After 11 months	$1,116	$1,146	$1,178	$1,210
18	After 12 months	$1,127	$1,161	$1,196	$1,231

Credit Card Procrastination worksheet

This worksheet has a title at the top, a column of labels (cells A3 through A18), and four columns of numeric constants and calculation results (cells B3 through E18).

To start, look at the example worksheet, identify the labels (all of which are in column A), and enter them into the worksheet. They are all too wide to fit in column A and will extend into the cells in column B.

Put mouse pointer here...

	A	B	C	D	E	F	G	H	I
1	The Cost of Credit Card Procrastination								
2									
3	Annual interest rate (%)								
4	Monthly interest rate								
5	Monthly multiplier								
6	Original amount ($)								
7	After 1 month								
8	After 2 months								
9	After 3 months								
10	After 4 months								
11	After 5 months								
12	After 6 months								
13	After 7 months								
14	After 8 months								
15	After 9 months								
16	After 10 months								
17	After 11 months								
18	After 12 months								
19									
20									

Worksheet labels

Changing the Width of a Column

Excel provides at least two ways to widen column A. One method involves selecting column A, opening the Format menu, and choosing the Column Width command. A dialog box appears in which you can set the width.

An alternate way to change the width of a column is to place the mouse pointer on the right border of the column heading ("A"). The mouse pointer turns into a vertical line with arrows pointing left and right. If you click and drag on the border with this mouse pointer, the column width adjusts as you move the mouse. You can widen column A until all the labels except the worksheet title (cell A1), fit comfortably in their cells.

...and drag column marker to here.

Column A widened

This worksheet contains five numeric constants. These constants control the results calculated on the worksheet. Four of the constants are annual interest rates (cells B3 through E3) of 12%, 15%, 18%, and 21%. These rates initially appear on the worksheet as decimals (.12, .15, .18, and .21). The fifth constant is the loan amount of $1,000 (cell B6).

Numeric constants in place

The remaining cells will hold the formulas that generate the detailed interest calculations. As you will see, Excel has outstanding features to help you create and copy formulas. These features minimize typing errors and save you time.

The Worksheet Formulas

Cells B4 through E4 will contain the values of the monthly interest rates. To compute the monthly rates, you divide the annual rates by 12. The cell locations, formulas, and expected results for these calculations are as follows:

Cell	Formula	Calculated Value
B4	=B3/12	0.01
C4	=C3/12	0.0125
D4	=D3/12	0.015
E4	=E3/12	0.0175

First, create the formula that goes into cell B4 and check the result that appears. The value 0.01 should appear in cell B4.

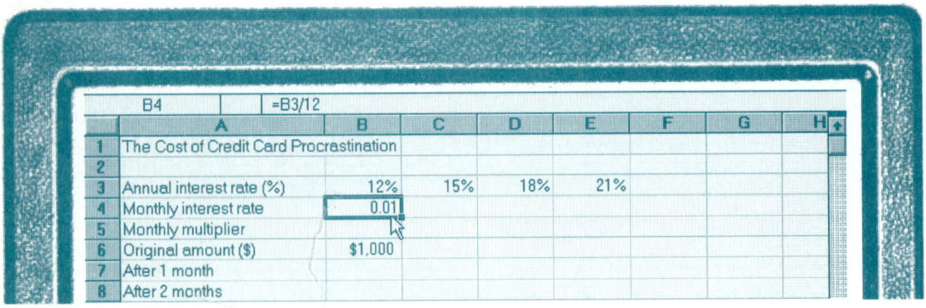

34   Simply Excel

Monthly interest formula in cell B4

Do not enter the remaining formulas directly. Instead, use the Excel Copy and Paste commands to copy the formula from cell B4 into cells C4 through E4.

When the first monthly interest rate formula is in cell B4, you can select that cell and use the Copy command on the Edit menu to copy the formula to the Clipboard. Then you can select the target cells (C4 through E4) into which to paste the original formula. Finally, choose the Paste command on the Edit menu.

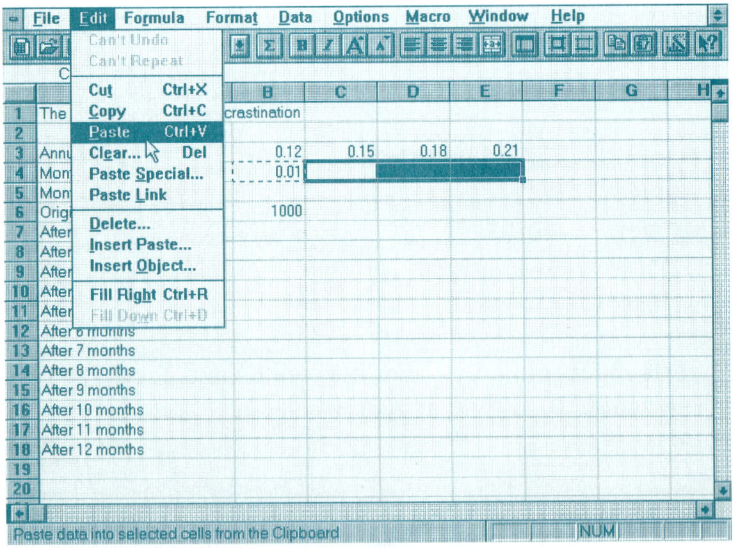

Copy and paste in process

When you finish this copy-and-paste operation, numeric values appear in cells C4 through E4. But the formulas in cells C4 through E4 no longer refer to cell B3! If you click each cell with a formula, the formula appears in the the formula bar.

Click this Cell	See this in Formula Bar
B4	=B3/12
C4	=C3/12
D4	=D3/12
E4	=E3/12

The formula in C4 refers to C3. Similarly, the formulas in cells D4 and E4 refer to D3 and E3, respectively. How is this possible?

Formula pasted into cells C4, D4, E4

When copying formulas, Excel looks at cell references in two ways: as relative references or as absolute references. Unless directed otherwise, Excel treats all cell references in formulas as *relative* to the location of the formula.

For example, Excel interprets the reference to cell B3 in the cell B4 formula as meaning "one cell above this formula." When you copy this formula from one cell to another, Excel changes the cell reference (B3) to match with the formula's new location.

In the credit card worksheet example, Excel changed the B3 reference to C3, D3, and E3 when the formula was copied into cells C4, D4, and E4, respectively. Since the formula contained a relative reference, Excel not only copied the formula, but also updated it to correspond to its three new locations.

An *absolute reference* is one you do not want Excel to change or update. You indicate that a cell reference is absolute by placing a dollar sign ($) in front of the row and column parts of the cell reference. Thus, if B3 were to be treated as an absolute reference, you would enter it as $B$3. If you copy a formula with an absolute reference, Excel will not change the reference to correspond to the formula's new location.

The two parts of a cell reference can be made absolute or relative independently. $B3 means that the column reference is absolute while the row reference is relative. Similarly, B$3 means that the column reference is relative while the row reference is absolute.

In a moment, you will see how this feature works as you enter the remaining formulas in the credit card worksheet.

Cells B5 through E5 need formulas that calculate the monthly interest multiplier. The formula for any one of these multipliers is computed by adding one to the monthly interest rate. The Excel formulas and cell locations for these calculations are as follows:

Cell	Formula
B5	=1 + B4
C5	=1 + C4
D5	=1 + D4
E5	=1 + E4

Taking a cue from the way you created the formulas for the monthly interest rates, first establish the formula for cell B5. Then copy and paste that formula into cells C5 through E5. Excel will adjust the relative cell reference in the formula to correspond to its three new locations.

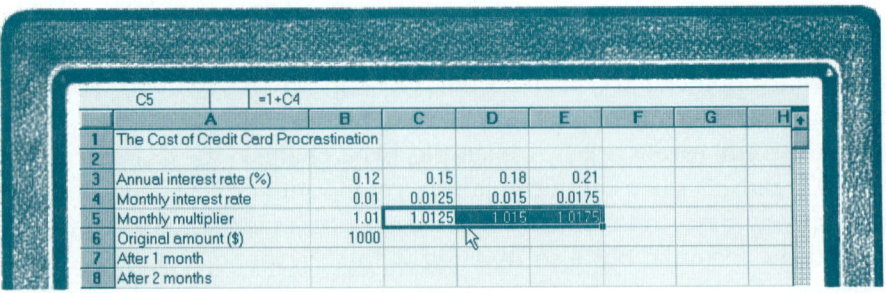

Monthly multiplier formulas in place

You now get a chance to create a formula with an absolute reference. Cell B6 contains a constant (1000). The same value appears in cells C6 through E6. You could simply copy the constant into these three locations or enter the same value three times. But if you did that, what would happen if you wanted to put a new amount into the worksheet to try a "what-if" scenario? You would have to enter the new value in four places.

A more elegant way to handle this situation is to put formulas into cells C6 through E6 that provide an absolute reference to the contents of cell B6. The appropriate formula is =$B6. If you enter this formula into cell C6 and then copy and paste the formula into cells D6 and E6, the value 1000 will appear in all four cell locations. If you later change the contents of cell B6, Excel automatically changes the contents of the other three cells.

	A	B	C	D	E
1	The Cost of Credit Card Procrastination				
2					
3	Annual interest rate (%)	0.12	0.15	0.18	0.21
4	Monthly interest rate	0.01	0.0125	0.015	0.0175
5	Monthly multiplier	1.01	1.0125	1.015	1.0175
6	Original amount ($)	1000	1000	1000	1000
7	After 1 month				
8	After 2 months				
9	After 3 months				

Original amount formulas in place

Now for the rest of the worksheet! What if you were told that you just needed to create one more formula to complete the worksheet? Is that possible?

It is with Excel. If you create a formula to calculate one month's interest accumulation, and use the proper mix of relative and absolute references, that formula will work when copied to all remaining worksheet cells.

To calculate the interest accumulation for cell B7, you could use the formula =B6*B$5. This formula takes the balance from the preceding period (B6) and multiplies it by the monthly multiplier (B$5). Putting this formula into cell B7 and copying it into the remaining cells in column B (B8 through B18) generates the interest accumulation for the first interest rate. We'll handle the extra decimal places of the results later with a formatting operation.

Simply Excel

[Spreadsheet screenshot showing cell B8 with formula =B7*B$5, columns A–E with rows 3–18 containing:]

	A	B	C	D	E
3	Annual interest rate (%)	0.12	0.15	0.18	0.21
4	Monthly interest rate	0.01	0.0125	0.015	0.0175
5	Monthly multiplier	1.01	1.0125	1.015	1.0175
6	Original amount ($)	1000	1000	1000	1000
7	After 1 month	1010			
8	After 2 months	1020.1			
9	After 3 months	1030.301			
10	After 4 months	1040.604			
11	After 5 months	1051.01			
12	After 6 months	1061.52			
13	After 7 months	1072.135			
14	After 8 months	1082.857			
15	After 9 months	1093.685			
16	After 10 months	1104.622			
17	After 11 months	1115.668			
18	After 12 months	1126.825			

First interest column calculated

In the formula in cell B7 the absolute row reference to the monthly multiplier (B$5), and the relative row reference to the previous period's amount (B6), let you apply this formula to every cell in column B. Will the same formula work for the other three columns? The formula's relative column references (B6, B$5) should make this feat possible. Let's try copying and pasting the B7 formula into the remaining cells, C7 through E18.

[Second spreadsheet screenshot showing cell C7 with formula =C6*C$5, with all columns B–E filled in:]

	A	B	C	D	E
1	The Cost of Credit Card Procrastination				
2					
3	Annual interest rate (%)	0.12	0.15	0.18	0.21
4	Monthly interest rate	0.01	0.0125	0.015	0.0175
5	Monthly multiplier	1.01	1.0125	1.015	1.0175
6	Original amount ($)	1000	1000	1000	1000
7	After 1 month	1010	1012.5	1015	1017.5
8	After 2 months	1020.1	1025.156	1030.225	1035.306
9	After 3 months	1030.301	1037.971	1045.678	1053.424
10	After 4 months	1040.604	1050.945	1061.364	1071.859
11	After 5 months	1051.01	1064.082	1077.284	1090.617
12	After 6 months	1061.52	1077.383	1093.443	1109.702
13	After 7 months	1072.135	1090.85	1109.845	1129.122
14	After 8 months	1082.857	1104.486	1126.493	1148.882
15	After 9 months	1093.685	1118.292	1143.39	1168.987
16	After 10 months	1104.622	1132.271	1160.541	1189.444
17	After 11 months	1115.668	1146.424	1177.949	1210.26
18	After 12 months	1126.825	1160.755	1195.618	1231.439

Remaining interest columns calculated

It worked! You created only four formulas for this worksheet. Excel's copy and paste features did the rest of the job. As you can see, the power of an electronic worksheet more than exceeds what is possible with paper, pencils, and a calculator.

If you have been building the credit card on your computer, this is a good time to save your worksheet. To do so, choose the Save command on the File menu. The Save As dialog box will appear. Name the worksheet file and save it to disk. For more information about naming, saving, and using Excel files, refer to Appendix C, "The Excel 4.0 Enviornment."

The final version of the Credit Card Procrastination worksheet has been reformatted and cleaned up. The Percent style in the toolbar's style box was used to change the format of cells B3 through E3. The Currency [0] style in the style box was used to reformat cells B6 through E18 and to round the amounts to whole dollars. Excel's border and pattern features were used to highlight various cell ranges.

Style box →

	A	B	C	D	E
1	The Cost of Credit Card Procrastination				
2					
3	Annual interest rate (%)	12%	15%	18%	21%
4	Monthly interest rate	0.01	0.0125	0.015	0.0175
5	Monthly multiplier	1.01000	1.01250	1.01500	1.01750
6	Original amount ($)	$1,000	$1,000	$1,000	$1,000
7	After 1 month	$1,010	$1,013	$1,015	$1,018
8	After 2 months	$1,020	$1,025	$1,030	$1,035
9	After 3 months	$1,030	$1,038	$1,046	$1,053
10	After 4 months	$1,041	$1,051	$1,061	$1,072
11	After 5 months	$1,051	$1,064	$1,077	$1,091
12	After 6 months	$1,062	$1,077	$1,093	$1,110
13	After 7 months	$1,072	$1,091	$1,110	$1,129
14	After 8 months	$1,083	$1,104	$1,126	$1,149
15	After 9 months	$1,094	$1,118	$1,143	$1,169
16	After 10 months	$1,105	$1,132	$1,161	$1,189
17	After 11 months	$1,116	$1,146	$1,178	$1,210
18	After 12 months	$1,127	$1,161	$1,196	$1,231

Credit Card Procrastination worksheet

You may wish to experiment with style changes on your own. If so, select the cells to be changed, open the style box menu by clicking the down arrow icon to the right of the style box, and choose one from the listed styles. To use Excel's pattern and border features, select the cell range to be changed, and use the Pattern and Border commands on the Format menu.

You will revisit the Excel worksheet environment in more detail later in this book. In the next chapter, you are invited to explore Excel's amazing chart features, which let you turn your electronic data into works of art.

Excel Charts

The Excel integrated spreadsheet package supports three key electronic number-crunching tools: worksheets, charts, and databases. In the previous chapter, you learned how to create worksheets, enter data and formulas, and format the results. You will now examine Excel's powerful charting tools, which let you turn data into beautiful and sophisticated graphs.

The Worksheet Data

Excel creates charts from data in a worksheet. For your charting explorations, you will use a simple worksheet of data on estimated revenues for multimedia products and services.

Since about 1985, multimedia has been a hot buzzword in the technology industries. Multimedia involves the integration of various devices (computers, videodisc players, CD-ROM drives, and display systems), media of all types (audio, video, text, and graphics), and software (graphical systems, browsing programs, and telecommunications). A multimedia product or service gives users interactive control of both hardware and software, and provides access to vast amounts of data and information.

	A	B	C	D	E	F	G	H	I
1		Estimated Multimedia Revenues							
2		(Dollars in Millions)							
3		1991	1992	1993	1994	1995	1996		
4	School	100	160	256	410	655	1049		
5	Home	100	220	484	1065	2343	5154		
6	Business	550	880	1408	2253	3604	5767		
7									
8									

Multimedia revenue data

Recent industry forecasts indicate that the demand for multimedia products and services will grow rapidly. When forecasts are converted into dollars, the results can look something like the worksheet of Estimated Multimedia Revenues.

Chapter 3: Excel Charts   43

The worksheet divides the revenues into three market categories: school, home, and business. The forecast is for a period of six years. The yearly data are in millions of dollars. The school segment grows from $100 million in 1991 to a little over $1 billion in 1996. The home market starts at $100 million and grows to a bit over $5 billion. The business segment ends up at slightly less than $6 billion, starting from a 1991 figure of $550 million.

The Excel ChartWizard

Excel provides several ways to transform data into charts. The easiest way to make a chart is to use the Excel ChartWizard. The ChartWizard tool is on the right end of the toolbar, immediately to the left of the Help tool. When activated, ChartWizard leads you through a few simple steps that produce a professional-looking chart.

To start the charting process, you select a range of data to be graphed. The selection may include labels. If labels are included, they will appear on the chart to identify the data.

On the multimedia worksheet, cells A3 through G6 have been selected for charting. After you have selected that data, you click the ChartWizard tool on the toolbar to activate Excel's charting feature.

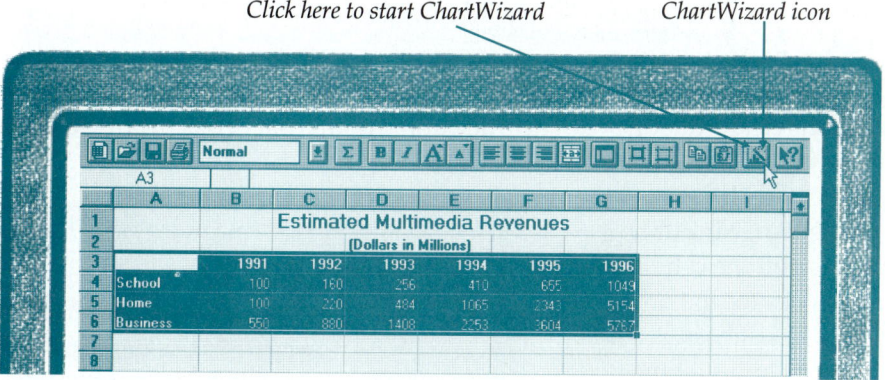

Data selected for charting

44 Simply Excel

Once you activate ChartWizard, a message on the status bar tells you to "Drag in document to create a chart." A dashed rectangle surrounds the selected data on the worksheet, and the dashes seem to move around the data like a bunch of marching ants.

You can go to any part of the worksheet and drag with the mouse to select a charting region. In the example, the region from cell A7 to cell I19 will be used for the chart. As you drag the mouse from A7 to I19, an outline appears on the screen.

Marching ants

Click inside A7 and drag to I19

Chart will appear inside this outline

When you release the mouse button, the outline disappears and you see a ChartWizard dialog box. The title bar indicates that this is the first of five steps you will take to create a chart.

The Range input box shows you the cell references for the data that will be charted. The range includes all the cells from A3 through G6. Note that the range formula contains only absolute cell references

ChartWizard dialog box

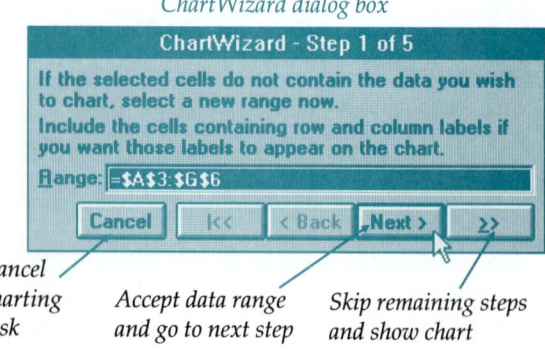

Cancel charting task

Accept data range and go to next step

Skip remaining steps and show chart

since both row and column identifiers are preceded by a dollar sign ($).

Note the active buttons along the bottom of the dialog box. You can use these to perform several tasks. The Cancel button lets you cancel the charting activities. The Next button

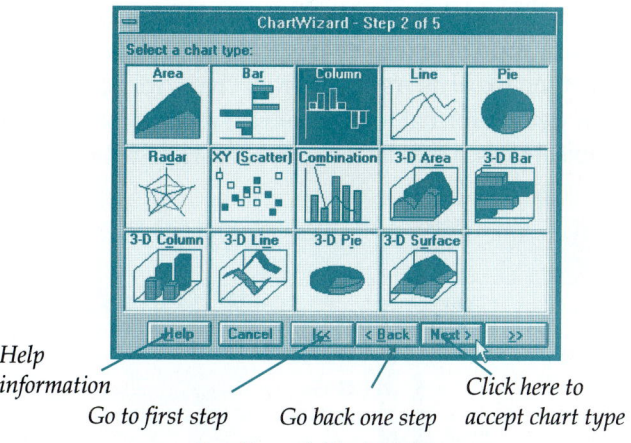

Help information
Go to first step *Go back one step* *Click here to accept chart type*
Excel's available chart types

tells the program to accept the current dialog box settings and values, and go to the next step. The "fast forward" button to the right of the Next button tells the program to skip any remaining steps and display the chart.

To accept the data range in the first dialog box, click the Next button. Clicking Next reveals the second ChartWizard dialog box, in which you can select the type of chart to be displayed.

Excel supports 14 different chart types, all of which appear on this dialog box. ChartWizard's default chart selection is a standard column chart. This selection, in the middle of the top row, is highlighted.

If you want to choose another type of chart, do so now by clicking the one you want. Note the new command buttons at the bottom of the dialog box. The Help button provides help information regarding the current step. You back up one step by using the Back button. The "rewind" button to the left of Back tells the program to return to the first step in the charting process.

To accept the selected chart type, click Next; a third ChartWizard dialog box appears. This box shows you the available column chart formats.

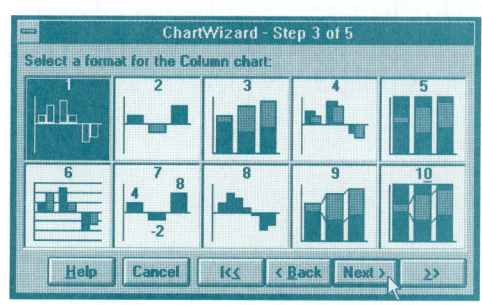

Possible formats for the column chart

46 Simply Excel

There are ten different display possibilities for Excel column charts. In fact, there are four to ten possible formats for each of Excel's 14 chart types. Altogether, Excel offers 86 different chart/format combinations.

The default format for the column chart is format number 1. Clicking Next tells Excel to use the selected format and also to bring up the fourth dialog box. This dialog box displays a sample chart based on the selections made so far. The radio buttons to the right of the sample chart indicate the ChartWizard's default interpretation of the data being plotted.

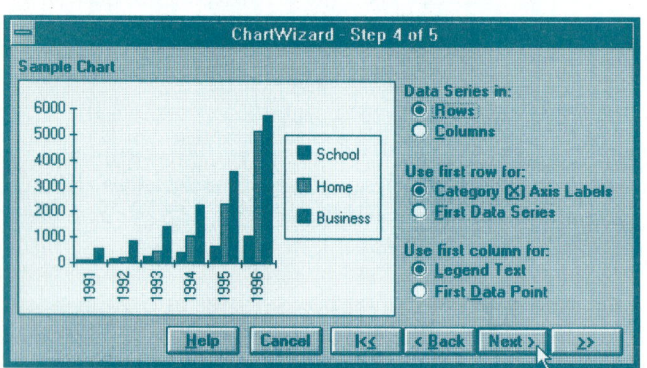

Chart preview and data interpretation settings

ChartWizard assumes that the data are arranged in rows and that the first row of data (years in this case) supplies the labels for the X axis, which is the line across the bottom of the chart.

ChartWizard also assumes that the first column of data is to be used for the legend. The legend, in the bordered rectangle to the right of the chart, identifies the three categories of charted data.

In this case, the ChartWizard's assumptions concerning the data are correct. If the assumptions were incorrect, you would use the radio buttons to help ChartWizard understand the data layout.

Clicking Next tells ChartWizard to proceed to the final dialog box.

The final dialog box lets you keep or remove the chart's legend. The two radio buttons in the upper-right corner of the dialog box control the legend display.

Chapter 3: Excel Charts   47

In the text input boxes underneath the legend radio buttons, you can add a title to the chart, and establish the titles for the X and Y axes. As you enter titles into the text input boxes, the titles appear on the sample chart.

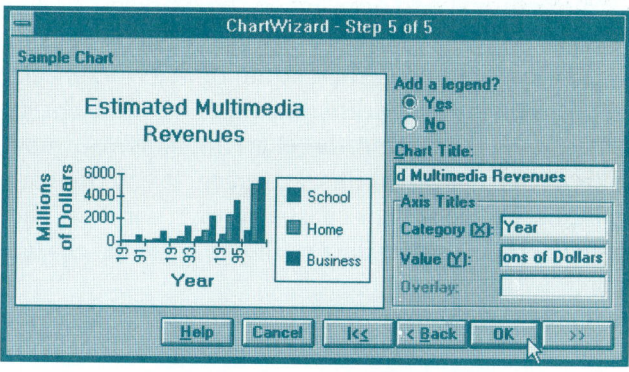

Legend, title, and axis label controls

Since this is the final step in the ChartWizard sequence, clicking OK tells the program to generate the chart, which will be based on the selections and settings in the five ChartWizard dialog boxes.

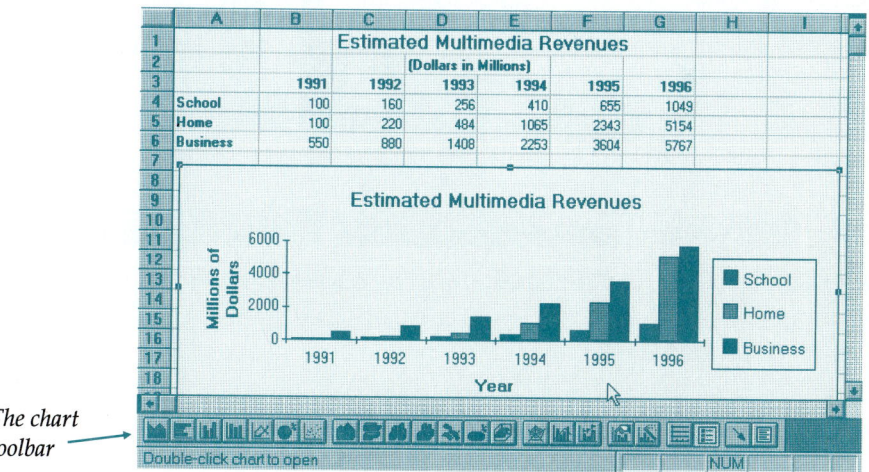

The chart toolbar

Chart created on the worksheet

Simply Excel

The column chart appears on the worksheet, filling the area you designated when you started using the ChartWizard. In addition, the chart toolbar appears along the bottom of the worksheet. You can use the tools on this toolbar to plot different versions of the chart quickly and easily.

Before you examine the chart toolbar, you may want to expand the column chart so that it fills the screen. If you double-click anywhere on the chart, Excel displays the chart in its own window. The expanded chart hides the worksheet and its data until you close the chart window.

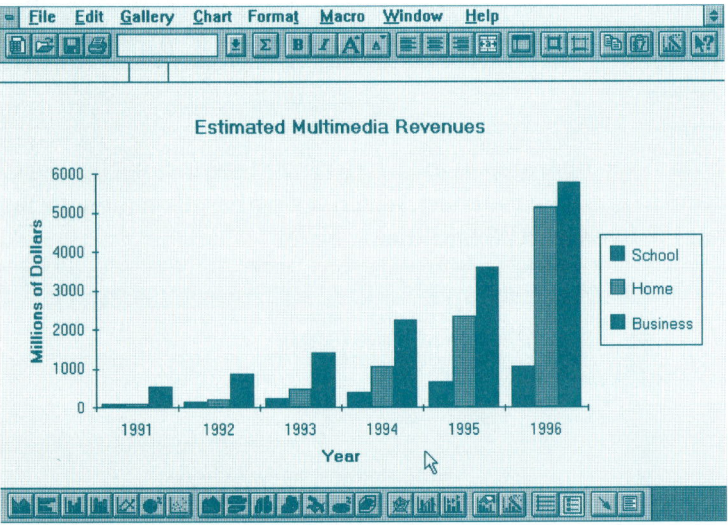

Chart expanded to fill the window

The Chart Toolbar

Most of the tools on this toolbar let you display the charted data in different chart formats. You activate these tools by clicking the icons on the left side of the toolbar.

Chapter 3: Excel Charts   **49**

The right end of the toolbar includes tools that let you place text boxes and arrows on a chart, and tools that let you change the display of chart legends and grid lines.

Click here to see an area chart

Chart toolbar

The first tool on the left is the area chart tool. This tool produces a composite graph of the worksheet data in the column chart. Instead of the data points being plotted in separate columns, they are stacked on top of each other to form sums for each period. Note that the Y-axis scale has doubled (from $6,000 million to $12,000 million) to accommodate the larger values.

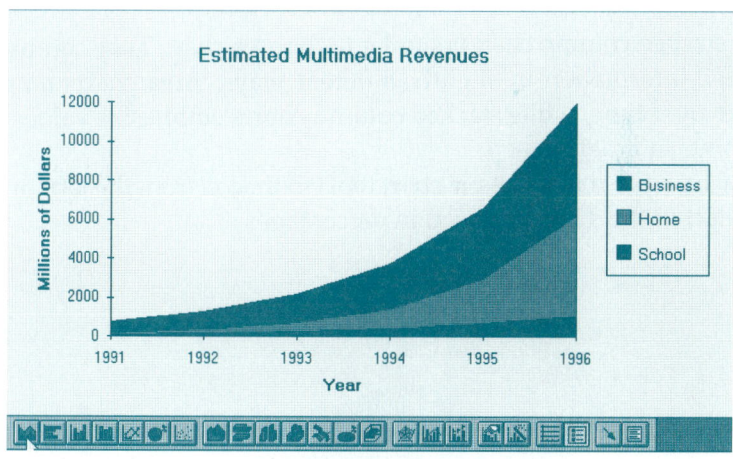

Area chart

Excel adjusts the look and scale of the chart automatically. You simply click an icon and the program performs the work.

Now let's try a stacked column chart. A click on the stacked column chart tool (fourth icon from the left) produces this display.

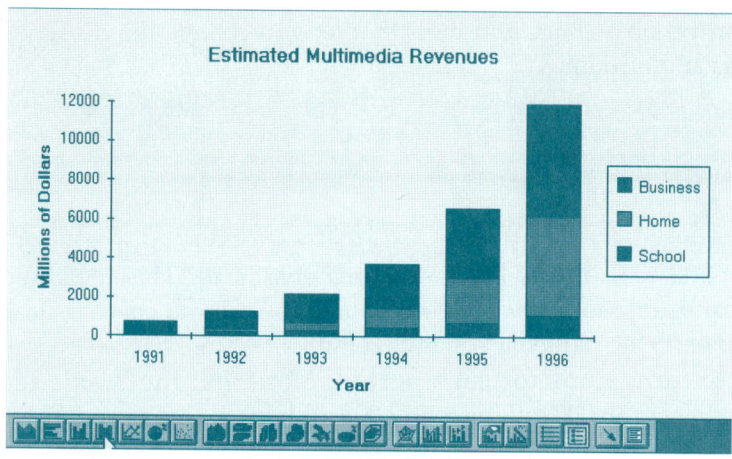

Stacked column chart

The stacked column chart is similar to the area chart. They communicate the same information in slightly different ways. Area charts emphasize changes over time, while stacked column charts emphasize values at specific points in time.

Now try a pie chart. The pie chart tool (sixth icon from the left) produces a pie chart of the data expressed in percentages

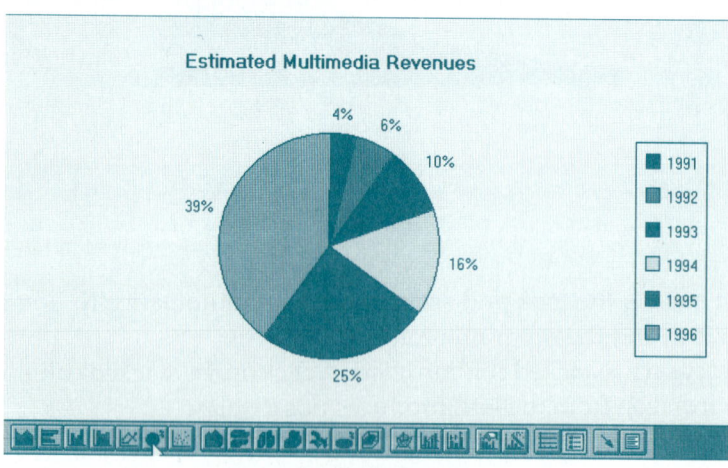

Pie chart with percentages

This chart displays the six years of revenues as pie-shaped slices of a circular graphic. Each slice is marked with a percentage figure. For example, you can see that 1995 sales made up 25 percent of the total sales. The legend now shows that the categories being charted are the annual total revenues rather than the three categories Business, Home, and School.

Here again, Excel and the chart tool automatically calculated the percentages, drew the chart, and relabeled the legend.

What happens if you click one of the 3-D charting tools? For example, try the 3-D area chart tool (eighth icon from the left).

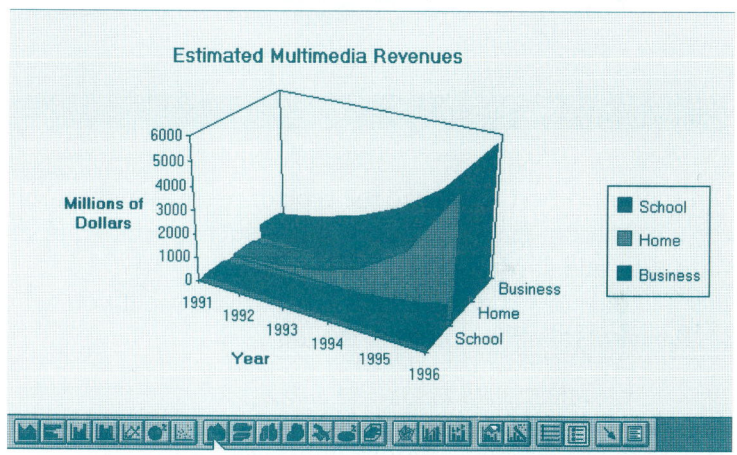

3-D area chart

If your computer has a color screen, you are probably saying something like "wow!" at this point. With the addition of perspective and color shading, the chart looks as if it pops up off the screen's surface.

Note that you could drop the legend from this chart since the market categories now appear along an axis. Clicking the legend tool (third icon from the right) removes or adds a chart's legend.

What other 3-D wonders does Excel have up its sleeve? Check out the results of the 3-D column chart tool (eleventh icon from the left).

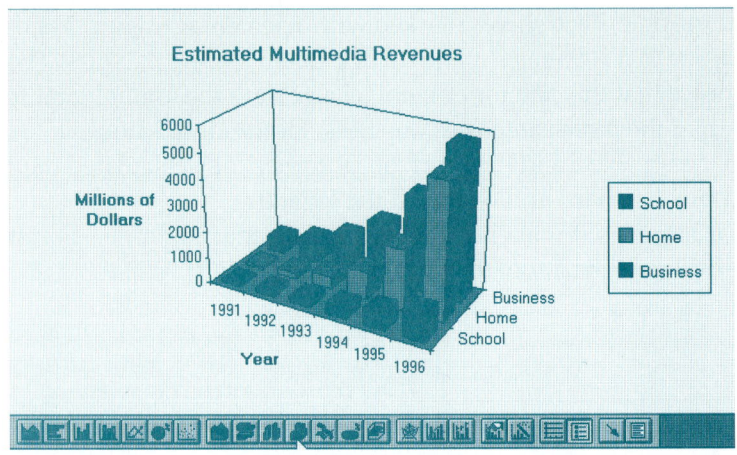

3-D column chart

The 3-D column chart looks like the type of professional charts you see in newspapers and magazines. Today, many such graphics are produced with computers and software products like Excel.

Excel's 3-D illusions continue. Here is what you see if you activate the 3-D line chart tool (twelfth icon from the left).

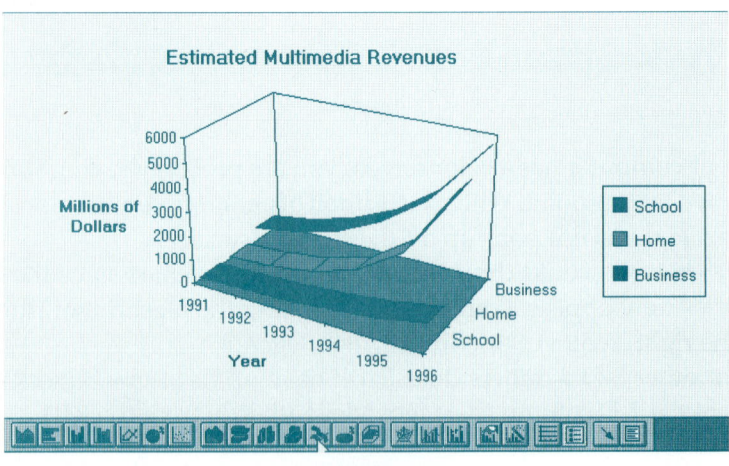

3-D line chart

In Chapter 6, you will explore some of the more advanced Excel chart features that let you change the orientation, perspective, and tilt of 3-D charts. For instance, this chart might look better if it were rotated slightly to the right. Excel has tools and features that let you change every element of a 3-D graph.

The 3-D pie chart tool (thirteenth icon from the left) produces charts that look like this.

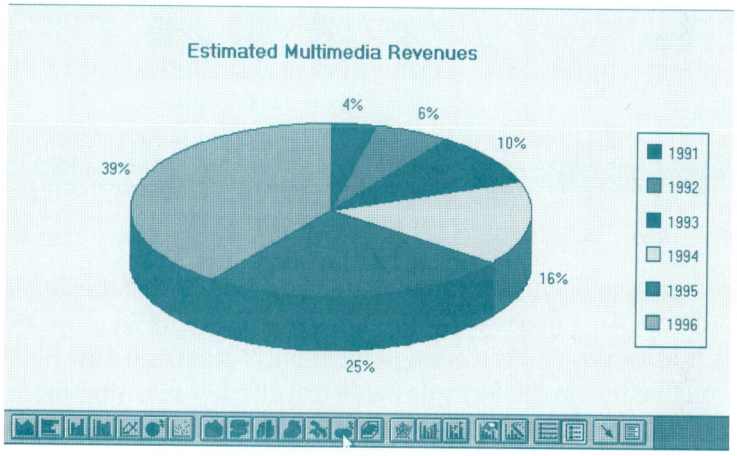

3-D pie chart with percentages

This chart looks somewhat like a thick version of the 2-D pie chart shown earlier. As on that pie chart, Excel displays percentages for each annual amount. By default, all of the pie slices fit together snugly. Excel has other 3-D pie chart formats in which the slices can be "exploded" away from the pie for emphasis.

In addition to the many standard chart options, Excel provides chart customization tools. For example, click the third icon from the left to restore the column chart. Then click the text box tool at the far right end of the chart toolbar.

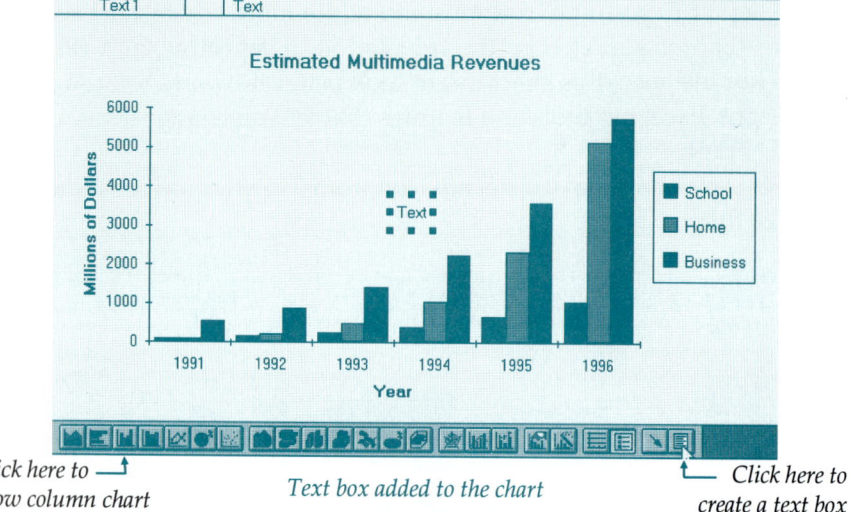

Click here to show column chart   *Text box added to the chart*   *Click here to create a text box*

A text box appears in the center of the chart, containing the default entry "Text." You can drag this text box anywhere on the chart window. When the text box is selected, you can change the default text inside the box ("Text") by editing that text in the formula bar. Excel also lets you alter the style and pattern of the box with the commands on the Format menu. The result is a custom note added to the chart.

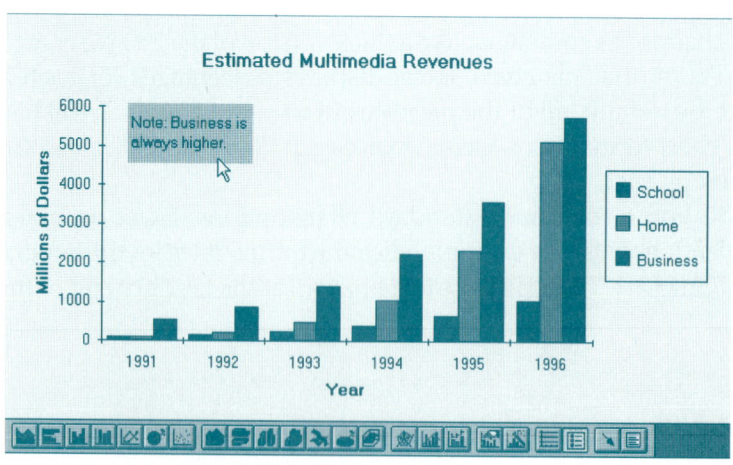

Chart with custom text box

Chapter 3: Excel Charts   **55**

The arrow tool lets you draw a line with an arrowhead anywhere on the chart. Suppose you want to associate the custom note with a particular chart feature. The solution is to use the arrow tool (second icon from right).

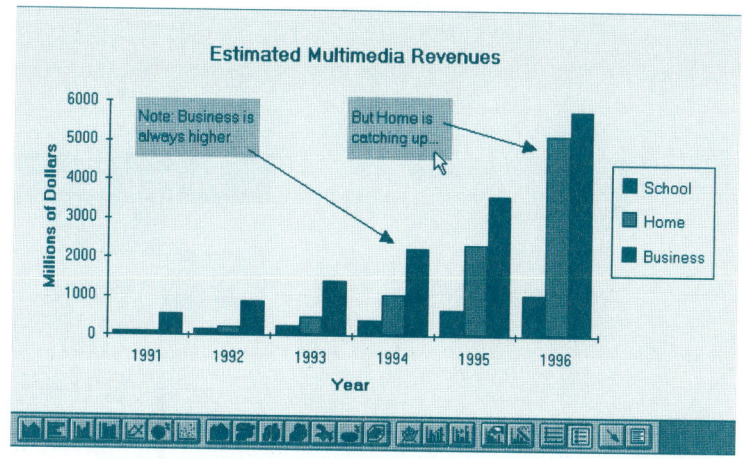

Chart with two custom notes and arrows

As with text boxes, you can move and adjust these arrows. Once you select an arrow, you can drag it to a new location, and you can adjust its length and orientation. You can use the text box and arrow tools to add several notes to a graph.

Excel's chart tools let people with practically no graphics experience create elegant and colorful charts. Special features, such as ChartWizard and the chart toolbar, streamline charting tasks. With Excel's ChartWizard, you can speedily produce and examine many different charts and chart options.

You have now looked at two of Excel's three major features: worksheets and charts. When you are ready, move on to the next chapter, where you will investigate Excel's database tools.

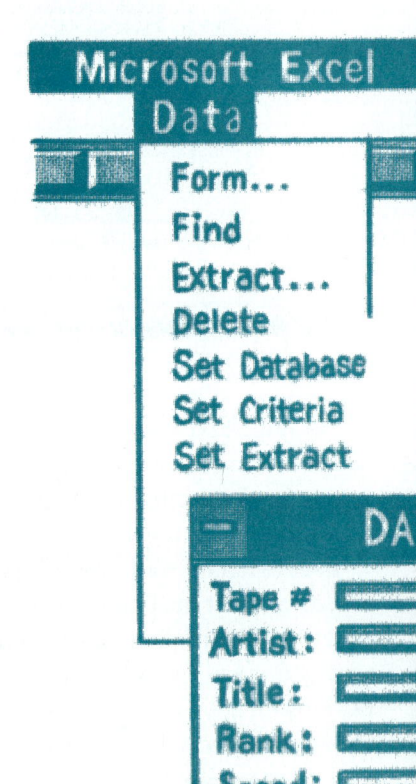

Excel Databases

4

You have now examined two of Excel's three primary calculation tools: worksheets and charts. In this chapter, you explore a third major Excel feature: databases. Excel's database tool helps you create, organize, and retrieve information that appears on a worksheet. You can use Excel to sort data and to search worksheets for specific entries. You can tell Excel to locate, extract, and print specific sets of data. If necessary, Excel can also help you with the statistical analysis of worksheet data sets.

Database Fundamentals

A *database* is any organized collection of data from which you can retrieve information. The majority of pages in a telephone book form a database of names, addresses, and telephone numbers. If you keep a log of automobile mileage records (miles driven, fuel consumed, costs), you are maintaining a simple database.

Electronic databases are like paper-and-pencil databases, but with several advantages. Electronic database systems can search through large amounts of data and quickly find specific entries. An electronic database can also very rapidly sort data in a variety of ways. Most importantly, in an electronic database you can include formulas that automatically compute results as part of the data.

Katy, a friend of the authors of this book, maintains a paper-and-pencil database with hundreds of Country and Western music titles and related dances. She has an extensive CD and cassette tape collection that she uses when she teaches Country and Western dancing and when she is a DJ at dance parties. She uses her database to locate songs and to organize the music for specific dances. Katy runs her dance business out of her home and already employs a computer to make flyers, to write letters, and to put together announcements. Recently, she has been investigating how she might use a package like Excel to help her with her music database tasks.

Chapter 4: Excel Databases   **59**

Katy ready for a class

For her cassette tape database, Katy keeps data entries on each song she has recorded. Her data entries show the tape number, artist name, song title, relative ranking (from 1, which means best, to 10, which means terrible), speed (fast, medium, slow), and up to three dances that can be done to the music. The primary dance is listed first.

For convenience, she has recorded one song on both sides of a single, short cassette. In this way, she can quickly load and play the music, and use fast-forward to set up the song for a replay.

Katy wants to create an electronic version of her big, and sometimes disorderly, paper-and-pencil database for cassettes. She begins by entering the information for her first 15 cassette tapes into an Excel worksheet.

	A	B	C	D	E	F	G	H
1			Country & Western Tape/Dance Database					
2	Tape #	Artist	Title	Rank	Speed	Dance 1	Dance 2	Dance 3
3	100	Eddie Raven	The Island	5	slow	Cha Cha		
4	101	Dwight Yoakam	Little Ways	3	medium	Two Step	Swing	
5	102	KT Oslin	Cornell Crawford	1	medium	Alley Cat	Horseshoe Special	Schottische
6	103	Hank Williams, Jr.	Born to Boogie	1	fast	Bocephus	Bonanza	Prancing Pony
7	104	Rockin Sydney	Jalapena Lena	1	fast	Flying 8	Two Step	Walkin Wazi
8	105	Kentucky Headhunters	Sixteen and Single	2	medium	Alley Cat	Schottische	Swing
9	106	Waylon Jennings	Lufenbach Texas	2	medium	Cha Cha		
10	107	Travis Tritt	Country Club	2	slow	Two Step	Horseshoe Special	Wooden Nickel
11	108	Garth Brooks	Not Counting You	2	medium	Two Step	Cowboy Boogie	Flying 8
12	109	Bellamy Brothers	Red Neck Girl	4	medium	Tush Push	Sixteen Step	Ten Step
13	110	Steve Warner	Lynda	1	fast	Walkin Wazi	Tush Push	Flying 8
14	111	Jerry Jeff Walker	Trashy Women	1	medium	Tush Push	Two Step	Flying 8
15	112	Hank Williams, Jr.	Old Habits	3	medium	Waltz		
16	113	Kathy Mattea	Going Gone	2	fast	Wooden Nickel	Two Step	Cha Cha
17	114	Mary Chapin Carpenter	Slow Country Dance	1	medium	Waltz		

Status bar hidden

Katy's Country & Western tape/dance worksheet

Katy created this example worksheet by entering the data for each cell and formatting the cells as shown in the illustration. She centered the data in columns A, D, and E. She right-justified the data in the remaining columns.

For this activity, Katy hid the status bar to make more room on the screen for the worksheet display. She did so by choosing the Workspace command on the Options menu, and selecting the setting that hides the bar.

In the database, Katy plans to have eight fields of information. The fields correspond to the eight columns shown on the worksheet. Each database field represents a specific, consistent kind of data that she plans to store and retrieve. Cells A2 through H2 contain the *field names* for the eight fields she plans to use.

Chapter 4: Excel Databases

Record — Field — Field name

	A	B	C	D	E	F	G	H
1			Country & Western Tape/Dance Database					
2	Tape #	Artist	Title	Rank	Speed	Dance 1	Dance 2	Dance 3
3	100	Eddie Raven	The Island	5	slow	Cha Cha		
4	101	Dwight Yoakam	Little Ways	3	medium	Two Step	Swing	
5	102	KT Oslin	Cornell Crawford	1	medium	Alley Cat	Horseshoe Special	Schottische
6	103	Hank Williams, Jr.	Born to Boogie	1	fast	Bocephus	Bonanza	Prancing Pony
7	104	Rockin Sydney	Jalapena Lena	1	fast	Flying 8	Two Step	Walkin Wazi
8	105	Kentucky Headhunters	Sixteen and Single	2	medium	Alley Cat	Schottische	Swing
9	106	Waylon Jennings	Lufenbach Texas	2	medium	Cha Cha		
10	107	Travis Tritt	Country Club	2	slow	Two Step	Horseshoe Special	Wooden Nickel
11	108	Garth Brooks	Not Counting You	2	medium	Two Step	Cowboy Boogie	Flying 8
12	109	Bellamy Brothers	Red Neck Girl	4	medium	Tush Push	Sixteen Step	Ten Step
13	110	Steve Warner	Lynda	1	fast	Walkin Wazi	Tush Push	Flying 8
14	111	Jerry Jeff Walker	Trashy Women	1	medium	Tush Push	Two Step	Flying 8
15	112	Hank Williams, Jr.	Old Habits	3	medium	Waltz		
16	113	Kathy Mattea	Going Gone	2	fast	Wooden Nickel	Two Step	Cha Cha
17	114	Mary Chapin Carpenter	Slow Country Dance	1	medium	Waltz		
18								
19								

Elements of a database

A row of cassette tape data on the worksheet forms a *record* of information for the database. For example, the data on row 3 is the first record in the database. Each database record contains the data for one complete database entry, separated into fields.

In an Excel database, every record must have the same number of fields (eight for this example), but fields within any specific record can be left empty. Katy does not have to put data into every field. For example, since only one dance works with the song "The Island," she left cells G3 and H3 empty in the first record.

Define the Database

To tell Excel that the worksheet data is to be treated as a database, Katy first selects the cells on the worksheet that will become the database. She includes in this selection the row of field names (row 2), and at least one blank row below the last data record. The cells she selects will define the *database range*.

62   Simply Excel

	A	B	C	D	E	F	G	H
1			Country & Western Tape/Dance Database					
2	Tape #	Artist	Title	Rank	Speed	Dance 1	Dance 2	Dance 3
3	100	Eddie Raven	The Island	5	slow	Cha Cha		
4	101	Dwight Yoakam	Little Ways	3	medium	Two Step	Swing	
5	102	K.T. Oslin	Cornell Crawford	1	medium	Alley Cat	Horseshoe Special	Schottische
6	103	Hank Williams, Jr.	Born to Boogie	1	fast	Bocephus	Bonanza	Prancing Pony
7	104	Rockin Sydney	Jalapena Lena	1	fast	Flying 8	Two Step	Walkin Wazi
8	105	Kentucky Headhunters	Sixteen and Single	2	medium	Alley Cat	Schottische	Swing
9	106	Waylon Jennings	Lurenbach Texas	2	medium	Cha Cha		
10	107	Travis Tritt	Country Club	2	slow	Two Step	Horseshoe Special	Wooden Nickel
11	108	Garth Brooks	Not Counting You	2	medium	Two Step	Cowboy Boogie	Flying 8
12	109	Bellamy Brothers	Red Neck Girl	4	medium	Tush Push	Sixteen Step	Ten Step
13	110	Steve Warner	Lynda	1	fast	Walkin Wazi	Tush Push	Flying 8
14	111	Jerry Jeff Walker	Trashy Women	1	medium	Tush Push	Two Step	Flying 8
15	112	Hank Williams, Jr.	Old Habits	3	medium	Waltz		
16	113	Kathy Mattea	Going Gone	2	fast	Wooden Nickel	Two Step	Cha Cha
17	114	Mary Chapin Carpenter	Slow Country Dance	1	medium	Waltz		
18								
19								
20								
21								

Database range

Selection to define database and database range

Excel needs the field names to help set up and perform its various database operations. It also needs a blank record at the bottom of the range to make room for later additions to the database.

```
Data
 Form...
 Find
 Extract...
 Delete
 Set Database
 Set Criteria
 Set Extract
 Sort...
 Series...
 Table...
 Parse...
 Consolidate...
 Crosstab...
```

Set Database command

After Katy selects the row of field names, the cells with data, and one or more blank rows, she chooses the Set Database command on the Data menu.

The Set Database command defines the selected cells as a database. When Katy chooses this command, the Data menu disappears and the screen shows the selected cells once again. The word "Database" appears in the formula bar to indicate that the selection now represents an Excel database.

Database Explorations

Katy wants to explore Excel's database features and discover what she can do with the organized electronic information.

Form command

You can control most Excel database operations by using commands on the Data menu. The first command, Form, lets Katy view, edit, and delete records from the database.

The Form Dialog Box

To see how the Form command works, Katy chooses Form on the Data menu. An Excel data form appears, enclosed in a dialog box. The program creates the form details specifically from the active database. The text areas on the form display the information for the first database record, which is tape 100.

Most databases let you display records in two ways: in a list view and in a form view. Excel's Form command shifts Katy from the list view (all records displayed on the worksheet) to the form view (a single record displayed on a data form in a dialog box).

Katy's field names for her database appear down the left side of the dialog box. In the text boxes next to the field names are the data entries for the first database record. The text boxes show the same information that appears on row 3 of the worksheet (record 1).

Form dialog box and first database record

In the upper-right corner of the dialog box, Katy sees the record number indicator. The indicator tells her that she is viewing the first of 15 records.

The buttons below the record number indicator give Katy control of several database activities. The top cluster of three buttons lets her add new records (New), delete existing records (Delete), and undo any edits she has made to the active record (Restore). The Restore button remains inactive until Katy edits or changes the data on the active record.

The three middle buttons allow Katy to browse through the database records and find previous records (Find Prev), find the next record (Find Next), and establish search criteria (Criteria) to find and display specific records. She can also browse through the database records by using the scroll bar near the middle of the dialog box.

The two bottom command buttons on the right remove the dialog box (Close) and give Katy access to Excel's help features (Help).

Browsing Through the Database

Katy clicks the Find Next button. Information for the second database record (tape 101) appears in the text boxes on the data form.

Katy continues to use the data form's browse controls (Find Prev and Find Next) to view all of the database records, one at a time. While browsing, she could edit the data by altering the information that appears on the form. When she either clicks a browse control (Find Prev, Find Next) or closes the dialog box (Close), changes she has made to data on the form get transferred to the worksheet. If she makes changes on the form that she does not wish to keep, she can click Restore to undo the edits and restore the original data for the active record.

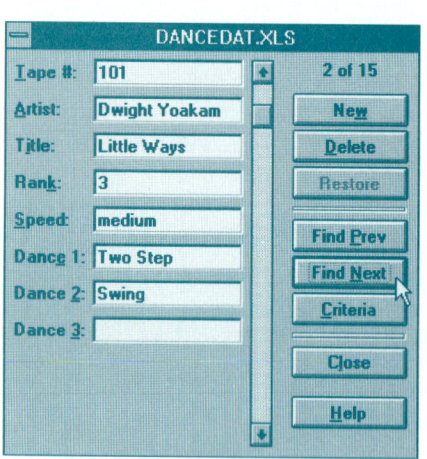

Second database record

The Search Criteria Feature

To use the data form to find specific records, Katy activates the dialog box's Criteria feature. When she clicks the Criteria button, she sees the following activities on the screen:

The data form clears.

The label "Criteria" replaces the record number indicator in the upper-right corner of the dialog box.

The caption on the Criteria button changes to "Form."

Once Katy enters criteria in the text boxes, clicking the Form button brings about the following actions:

The data form display replaces the criteria form.

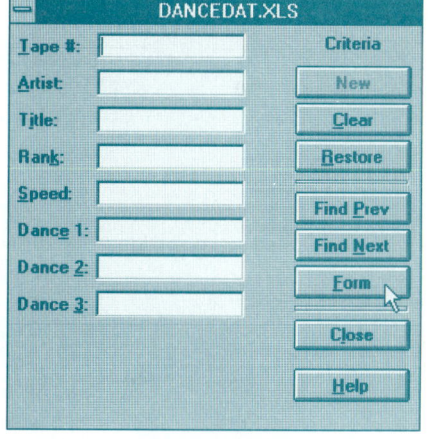

The criteria form

The records that match the criteria are ready to be viewed with the browse controls.

Katy enters a search criterion

Katy wants to search the database and find all the records that list "Two Step" in the Dance 1 field. She often has to make this search for a specific dance when she is teaching a class or preparing a play list for a party. She enters **Two Step** into the Dance 1 field on the criteria form.

In this case, she enters the two words using initial capital letters. Excel is *case insensitive* when performing searches. That is, the program ignores capitalization.

The search criterion "Two Step" will find all records with those words in the Dance 1 field, no matter how the words are capitalized. If there are records with "two step," "tWo sTep," or "TWO STEP" in the Dance 1 field, they will be found when Katy searches the database.

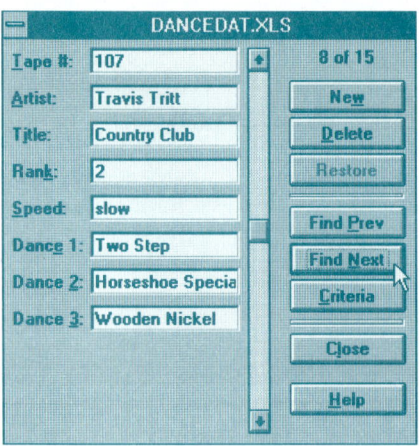

Record of tape 107 found

After she enters the criterion, Katy clicks the Form button and returns to the data form view. The form shows the record for tape 101, the record she was viewing when she activated the criteria feature. This record happens to have "Two Step" in the Dance 1 field.

When returning to the data form from the criteria form, Excel always displays the record that was in view when the Criteria button was clicked. This displayed record may or may not match the criterion. To fully activate Excel's find features, Katy has to click one of the browse controls (Find Prev or Find Next).

Browse controls

Katy clicks the Find Next button. The display on the data form shifts to record 8 (tape 107). Excel skips over records 3 through 7 (rows 5 through 9) since they do not satisfy the search criterion—those records do not have "Two Step" in the Dance 1 field.

Katy clicks the Find Next button again. The data for record 9 (tape 108) appears. This is the last record that satisfies the search criterion. If Katy clicks Find Next again, the program beeps to tell her that she is at the end of the database.

Excel has located all three records that correspond to Katy's search criterion. While the criteria feature remains active, the Find buttons narrow the display of found records to only the records that meet the criterion. All other records are ignored.

Katy wants to narrow the search even more. She clicks the Criteria button to return to the criteria form.

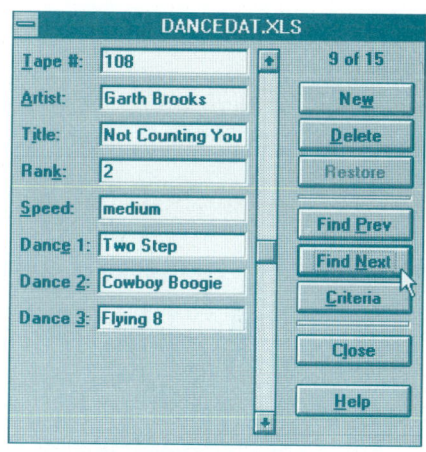

Record of tape 108 found

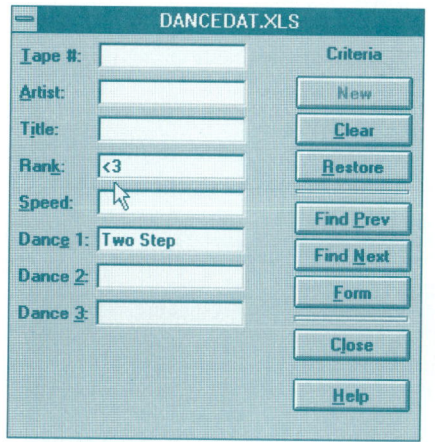

Katy enters a second search criterion

Her Dance 1 criterion entry remains in place ("Two Step"). She enters a second search criterion into the Rank field. The entry (<3) tells Excel to alter the search to find only matching records that have a "rank of less than 3." Katy uses this type of search to find the best possible pieces of music (with a rank of less than 3) for the dance ("Two Step") she plans to do.

After Katy enters this second criterion and returns to the data form view, she discovers two records that meet her new criteria. The Find buttons display the data for tapes 107 and 108. These are the only two database entries that have "Two Step" in the Dance 1 field and a music ranking of less than 3.

You can use six comparison operators, like the "less than" symbol (<), to define search criteria. Those operators are as follows:

68 Simply Excel

Operator	Meaning
=	Equal to
>	Greater than
<	Less than
>=	Greater than or equal to
<=	Less than or equal to
<>	Not equal to

To deactivate the criteria feature, all Katy has to do is either close the Form dialog box or clear the criteria entries on the criteria form view.

Katy closes the dialog box by clicking the Close button. She will use the Form command again a bit later in this chapter, but now she wants to look at Excel's database sorting features.

The Sort Feature

To activate the Excel sort feature, Katy first selects the range of data that she wants to sort (cells A3 through H19). When sorting a database, the sort

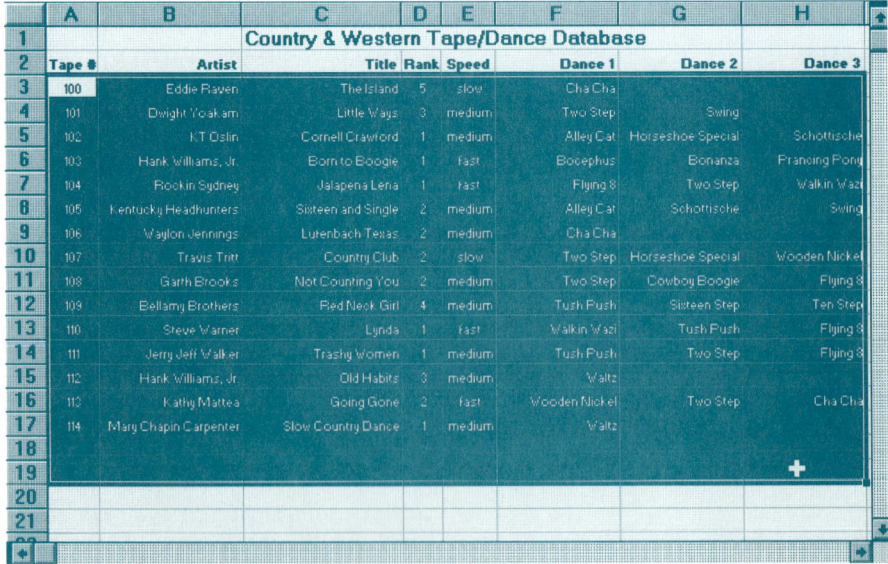

Database range to be sorted

range should include only database records and not the row of field names (row 2 in this case).

Once she selects the database sort range, Katy chooses the Sort command on the Data menu.

A Sort dialog box appears. This box lets Katy control whether rows or columns will be sorted, and lets her specify the *sort keys* to be used. For an Excel database, the sort normally operates by rows of data (by records).

In this case, the sort keys determine which columns of data are used to direct the sort. The default entry in the 1st Key field, $A$3, points to the entries in

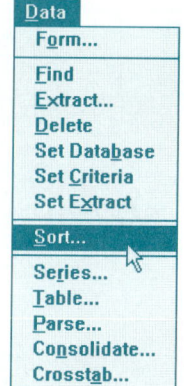

Sort command on the Data menu

column 1, the Tape # field. The data in this column are already sorted in ascending order. To reverse this order, Katy clicks the Descending option button for the 1st Key, and then clicks OK to perform the sort.

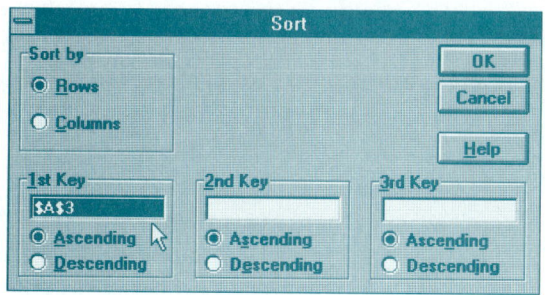

Sort dialog box

The records now appear in reverse order by tape number. Tape 114 is first and tape 100 is at the bottom of the list.

70 Simply Excel

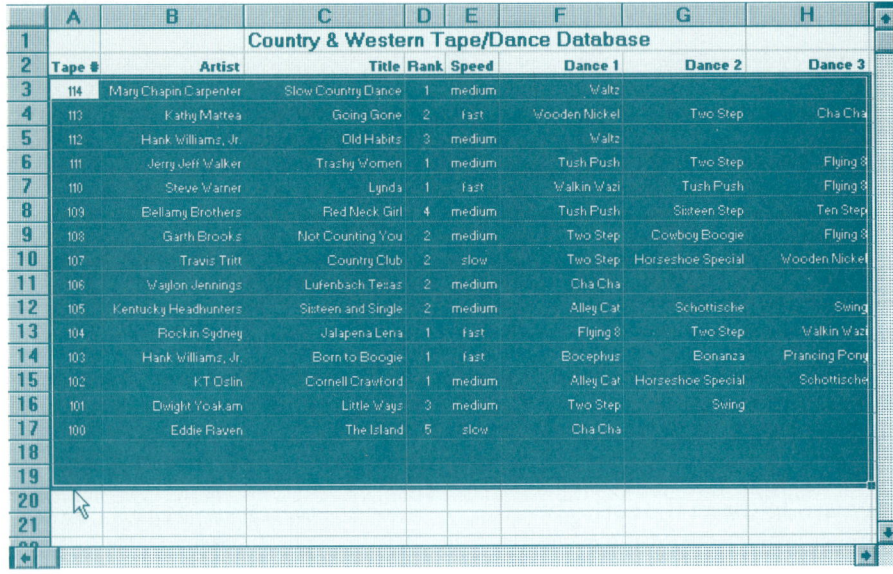

Data sorted in descending order by tape number

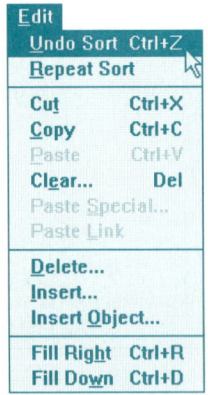

Katy uses the Undo Sort command

As Excel sorts the data in column A (the Tape # field), it moves the data in the other seven fields on the records to match the new record locations. In other words, Excel keeps the information for each record together as the sort occurs. For the small database in this example, the 120 fields of data move faster than the eye can see.

There are several ways to put the database back in its original order. One way is for Katy to do an ascending sort on the Tape # field. Another way is for her to use the Undo Sort command on the Edit menu.

The Undo Sort command lets Katy reverse the effects of the previous Sort command. In this case, when she chooses Undo Sort, the database returns to its original order.

Now Katy wants to sort the database in descending order (slow, medium, fast) using the Speed field. She often needs to view her music data in this way so that she can easily find good slow tunes for teaching, and "smoking" fast tunes for dance demonstrations. She once again chooses the Sort command on the Data menu.

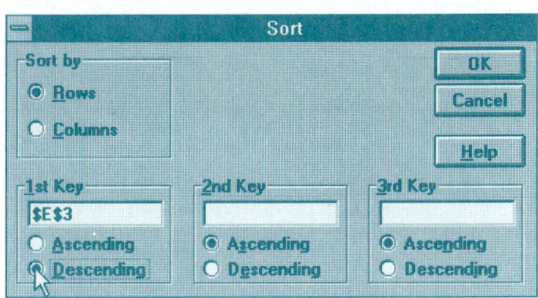

Specifying a sort on the Speed field

When the Sort dialog appears, Katy changes the 1st Key to $E$3 to direct the sort onto the Speed field. If she sorts the tapes by speed in ascending order, the tapes marked "fast" would appear first, then the tapes marked "medium," and then the tapes marked "slow." She clicks the Descending

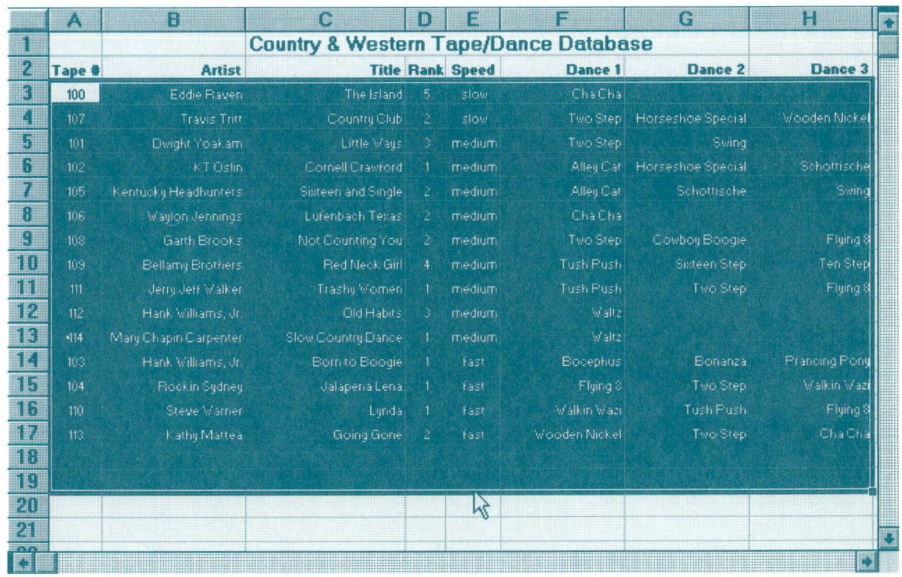

Data sorted in descending order by speed

option button to force the tapes marked "slow" to the top of the list. Once she makes these selections, she clicks OK to activate the sort.

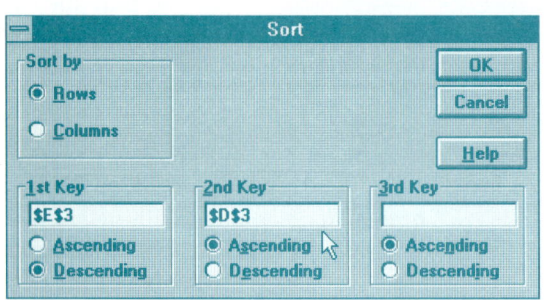

Specifying a sort on the Speed and Rank fields

Katy notices that although the tape records are rearranged and the tape speeds are in order, the rankings remain jumbled. She decides to try a two-key sort that will sort the records by both tape speed and rank. She brings up the Sort dialog box and enters the following sort key information.

She tells Excel to use the Speed column ($E$3) as the first key, and to sort that field in descending order. She then tells Excel to use the Rank column ($D$3) in ascending order as the second sort key. She clicks OK to perform the indicated sort.

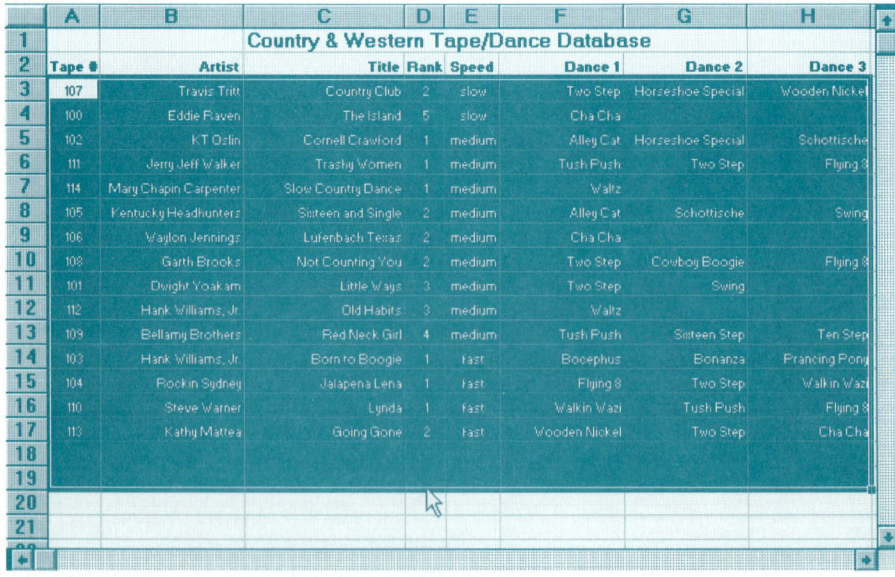

Result of the two-key sort operation

Chapter 4: Excel Databases 73

Excel responds instantly. The database is re-sorted with the Speed fields in descending order and the associated Rank fields in ascending order. Even with a lot of effort, this type of sort is often impossible with Katy's old paper-and-pencil database system.

When Katy asks Excel to perform a sort that involves two sort keys, the program starts by sorting the data using the first sort key. When that sort is complete, Excel then sorts records with the same entry in the first sort field according to the second sort key.

In Katy's example, Excel sorted the records using the Speed field (slow, medium, fast). The program then sorted all the records marked "slow" using the Rank field as the secondary sort key. The same secondary sort was applied to the records marked "medium" and to the records marked "fast."

Katy feels adventurous and decides she wants to try a three-key sort. She chooses the Sort command on the Data menu to bring up the Sort dialog box. She tells Excel to use the Dance 1 field ($F$3) as the first key (ascending order), Speed ($E$3) as the second key (descending order), and Rank ($D$3) as the third key (ascending order). She clicks OK to activate the sort.

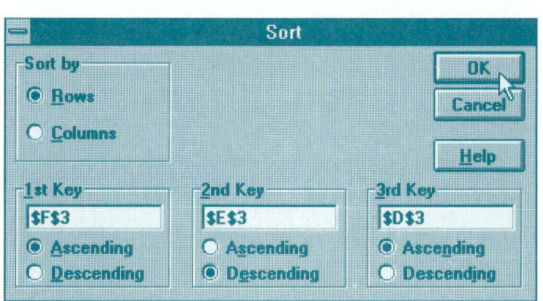

Sort dialog box for three-dey sort

Excel sorts the database using the threekeys. The result: a database where the Dance 1 fields are in alphabetical order, with each group of dances then sorted by speed and rank. Katy knows she can routinely use this type of ordering each day in her dance business. Being able to sort her music information in a variety of ways will make her class preparation tasks easier and more efficient.

What happened to the original database after all these sorting activities? The answer is that all the data are still there and you can quickly restore the original database. To put the database back in its original order, Katy tells Excel to perform a single-key, ascending sort on the Tape # field.

If you have been following these database explorations on your computer, restore your version of the database to its original form. Use the Sort

	A	B	C	D	E	F	G	H
1		Country & Western Tape/Dance Database						
2	Tape #	Artist	Title	Rank	Speed	Dance 1	Dance 2	Dance 3
3	102	KT Oslin	Cornell Crawford	1	medium	Alley Cat	Horseshoe Special	Schottische
4	105	Kentucky Headhunters	Sixteen and Single	2	medium	Alley Cat	Schottische	Swing
5	103	Hank Williams, Jr.	Born to Boogie	1	fast	Bocephus	Bonanza	Prancing Pony
6	100	Eddie Raven	The Island	5	slow	Cha Cha		
7	106	Waylon Jennings	Lutenbach Texas	2	medium	Cha Cha		
8	104	Rockin Sydney	Jalapena Lena	1	fast	Flying 8	Two Step	Walkin Waz
9	111	Jerry Jeff Walker	Trashy Women	1	medium	Tush Push	Two Step	Flying 8
10	109	Bellamy Brothers	Red Neck Girl	4	medium	Tush Push	Sixteen Step	Ten Step
11	107	Travis Tritt	Country Club	2	slow	Two Step	Horseshoe Special	Wooden Nickel
12	108	Garth Brooks	Not Counting You	2	medium	Two Step	Cowboy Boogie	Flying 8
13	101	Dwight Yoakam	Little Ways	3	medium	Two Step	Swing	
14	110	Steve Warner	Lynda	1	fast	Walkin Wazi	Tush Push	Flying 8
15	114	Mary Chapin Carpenter	Slow Country Dance	1	medium	Waltz		
16	112	Hank Williams, Jr.	Old Habits	3	medium	Waltz		
17	113	Kathy Mattea	Going Gone	2	fast	Wooden Nickel	Two Step	Cha Cha

Result of the two-key sort

command on the Data menu and sort the Tape # field (column A) back to ascending order.

Also, you might want to save a copy of the database by using the Save command on the File menu.

Adding a Database Record

One easy way to add a record to a database is to use the Form command. Katy chooses that command on the Data menu. When the Form dialog box appears, she clicks the New button to tell Excel that she wants to add a new record.

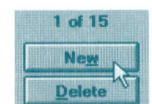

New button in the Form Dialog box

The data form clears and Katy enters the data for a new record into the text boxes. As she completes an entry for each field, she uses the TAB key to move the cursor to the next text box.

When she completes the data entry for a new record, she can click either Close or New to record the data. If she were going to enter more records,

Chapter 4: Excel Databases 75

she would click New. Since she only wants to enter this one new record, she clicks Close to add the new record and remove the dialog box.

Excel updates the database with the new record (tape 115). The program automatically inserts new records at the bottom of the database range.

This example exploration of Excel's database features convinces Katy to trade in her old paper-and-pencil system. An electronic database like Excel's lets her quickly and efficiently create, organize, and search her cassette tape data records. Katy realizes that Excel will also help her organize her CD

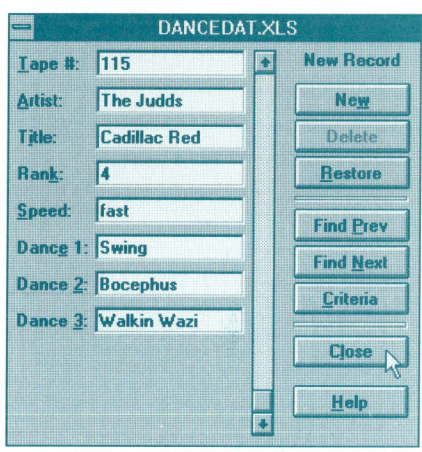

Katy adds a new record

Tape #	Artist	Title	Rank	Speed	Dance 1	Dance 2	Dance 3
		Country & Western Tape/Dance Database					
100	Eddie Raven	The Island	5	slow	Cha Cha		
101	Dwight Yoakam	Little Ways	3	medium	Two Step	Swing	
102	KT Oslin	Cornell Crawford	1	medium	Alley Cat	Horseshoe Special	Schottische
103	Hank Williams, Jr.	Born to Boogie	1	fast	Bocephus	Bonanza	Prancing Pony
104	Rockin Sydney	Jalapena Lena	1	fast	Flying 8	Two Step	Walkin Wazi
105	Kentucky Headhunters	Sixteen and Single	2	medium	Alley Cat	Schottische	Swing
106	Waylon Jennings	Lufenbach Texas	2	medium	Cha Cha		
107	Travis Tritt	Country Club	2	slow	Two Step	Horseshoe Special	Wooden Nickel
108	Garth Brooks	Not Counting You	2	medium	Two Step	Cowboy Boogie	Flying 8
109	Bellamy Brothers	Red Neck Girl	4	medium	Tush Push	Sixteen Step	Ten Step
110	Steve Warner	Lynda	1	fast	Walkin Wazi	Tush Push	Flying 8
111	Jerry Jeff Walker	Trashy Women	1	medium	Tush Push	Two Step	Flying 8
112	Hank Williams, Jr.	Old Habits	3	medium	Waltz		
113	Kathy Mattea	Going Gone	2	fast	Wooden Nickel	Two Step	Cha Cha
114	Mary Chapin Carpenter	Slow Country Dance	1	medium	Waltz		
115	The Judds	Cadillac Red	4	fast	Swing	Bocephus	Walkin Wazi

New record in the database

collection (with multiple titles on each disc), and will help her with many of her general dance business activities.

This chapter introduced some basic features of the Excel database tool. You will learn more about databases later in this book. For now, move on to the next chapter. There, you will discover new Excel worksheet features to help you handle more complex calculation tasks.

Worksheet Magic

5

Excel provides many powerful tools to help you build and use worksheets. In this chapter, you will explore a few such tools, including some that let you insert, delete, and copy entire groups of cells. You will discover how Excel can help you locate cells containing specific types of information, such as all the cells on a worksheet that have formulas. You will also learn how to use Excel to create entire rows or columns of data automatically, almost like magic.

Excel Edit Commands

As you plan and build worksheets, you will eventually need to either delete or insert cells. Excel anticipates this need by providing Delete and Insert commands on the Edit menu.

Remember the Credit Card Procrastination worksheet from Chapter 2? Let's use a version of that worksheet to explore the Delete and Insert commands. If you wish to follow this example on your computer, use the credit card worksheet that you created and saved in Chapter 2. If you have a copy of the Simply Excel Convenience Disk, you can also load the worksheet from that disk.

	A	B	C	D	E	F	G	H
1	The Cost of Credit Card Procrastination							
2								
3	Annual interest rate (%)	12%	15%	18%	21%			
4	Monthly interest rate	0.01	0.0125	0.015	0.0175			
5	Monthly multiplier	1.01	1.0125	1.015	1.0175			
6	Original amount ($)	$1,000	$1,000	$1,000	$1,000			
7	After 1 month	$1,010	$1,013	$1,015	$1,018			
8	After 2 months	$1,020	$1,025	$1,030	$1,035			
9	After 3 months	$1,030	$1,038	$1,046	$1,053			
10	After 4 months	$1,041	$1,051	$1,061	$1,072			
11	After 5 months	$1,051	$1,064	$1,077	$1,091			
12	After 6 months	$1,062	$1,077	$1,093	$1,110			
13	After 7 months	$1,072	$1,091	$1,110	$1,129			
14	After 8 months	$1,083	$1,104	$1,126	$1,149			
15	After 9 months	$1,094	$1,118	$1,143	$1,169			
16	After 10 months	$1,105	$1,132	$1,161	$1,189			
17	After 11 months	$1,116	$1,146	$1,178	$1,210			
18	After 12 months	$1,127	$1,161	$1,196	$1,231			
19								
20								

Credit Card Procrastination worksheet

The credit card worksheet shows the account balances as the interest accumulates on $1,000 at four different interest rates (12%, 15%, 18%, and 21%). There are five numeric constants on this worksheet: the four annual interest rates on row 3 (cells B3 through E3), and an original amount of $1,000 in cell B6.

The Delete Command

Suppose you wanted to delete all the information in column D (the 18% column). You could do so in several ways. One way would be to select all the cells in that column and use the Clear command on the Edit menu. The result would be an empty column of cells between columns C and E. There are times when you do want to clear entire cell ranges like this and not disturb the layout of the remaining cells. The Clear command lets you perform this type of editing operation.

	A	B	C	D	E
1	The Cost of Credit Card Procrastination				
2					
3	Annual interest rate (%)	12%	15%		21%
4	Monthly interest rate	0.01	0.0125		0.0175
5	Monthly multiplier	1.01	1.0125		1.0175
6	Original amount ($)	$1,000	$1,000		$1,000
7	After 1 month	$1,010	$1,013		$1,018
8	After 2 months	$1,020	$1,025		$1,035
9	After 3 months	$1,030	$1,038		$1,053
10	After 4 months	$1,041	$1,051		$1,072
11	After 5 months	$1,051	$1,064		$1,091
12	After 6 months	$1,062	$1,077		$1,110
13	After 7 months	$1,072	$1,091		$1,129
14	After 8 months	$1,083	$1,104		$1,149
15	After 9 months	$1,094	$1,118		$1,169
16	After 10 months	$1,105	$1,132		$1,189
17	After 11 months	$1,116	$1,146		$1,210
18	After 12 months	$1,127	$1,161		$1,231
19					
20					

Cells cleared with the Edit menu's Clear command

Another option would be to select all the cells in column D and use the Delete command on the Edit menu. Doing so produces an interesting result.

Simply Excel

First, select all of the cells in column D by clicking the column D label at the top of the worksheet. All the cells in column D will become highlighted.

	A	B	C	D	E	F	G	H
1	The Cost of Credit Card Procrastination							
2								
3	Annual interest rate (%)	12%	15%	18%	21%			
4	Monthly interest rate	0.01	0.0125	0.015	0.0175			
5	Monthly multiplier	1.01	1.0125	1.015	1.0175			
6	Original amount ($)	$1,000	$1,000	$1,000	$1,000			
7	After 1 month	$1,010	$1,013	$1,015	$1,018			
8	After 2 months	$1,020	$1,025	$1,030	$1,035			
9	After 3 months	$1,030	$1,038	$1,046	$1,053			
10	After 4 months	$1,041	$1,051	$1,061	$1,072			
11	After 5 months	$1,051	$1,064	$1,077	$1,091			
12	After 6 months	$1,062	$1,077	$1,093	$1,110			
13	After 7 months	$1,072	$1,091	$1,110	$1,129			
14	After 8 months	$1,083	$1,104	$1,126	$1,149			
15	After 9 months	$1,094	$1,118	$1,143	$1,169			
16	After 10 months	$1,105	$1,132	$1,161	$1,189			
17	After 11 months	$1,116	$1,146	$1,178	$1,210			
18	After 12 months	$1,127	$1,161	$1,196	$1,231			
19								
20								

Column D cells selected

When you have selected the cells to be deleted, open the Edit menu and choose the Delete command.

After you choose Delete, Excel does three things:

1. Deletes the information in all cells of the selected column.

2. Saves the deleted information in memory so you can restore it by using the Undo command.

3. Moves the information in column E cells to column D.

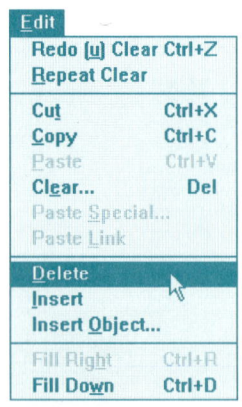

The Edit menu's Delete command

Chapter 5: Worksheet Magic

	A	B	C	D	E
1	The Cost of Credit Card Procrastination				
2					
3	Annual interest rate (%)	12%	15%	21%	
4	Monthly interest rate	0.01	0.0125	0.0175	
5	Monthly multiplier	1.01	1.0125	1.0175	
6	Original amount ($)	$1,000	$1,000	$1,000	
7	After 1 month	$1,010	$1,013	$1,018	
8	After 2 months	$1,020	$1,025	$1,035	
9	After 3 months	$1,030	$1,038	$1,053	
10	After 4 months	$1,041	$1,051	$1,072	
11	After 5 months	$1,051	$1,064	$1,091	
12	After 6 months	$1,062	$1,077	$1,110	
13	After 7 months	$1,072	$1,091	$1,129	
14	After 8 months	$1,083	$1,104	$1,149	
15	After 9 months	$1,094	$1,118	$1,169	
16	After 10 months	$1,105	$1,132	$1,189	
17	After 11 months	$1,116	$1,146	$1,210	
18	After 12 months	$1,127	$1,161	$1,231	

Worksheet after delete operation

Excel deletes the contents of cells in column D and closes up the space on the worksheet. The information that was in column E now sits in column D.

Besides moving the column E information to column D, Excel adjusted all the relative cell references in the formulas that were in column E. The program assumed that you wanted the formulas it moved to produce the same results in column D that they produced in column E, and automatically adjusted the formulas to match their new column D locations.

The Undo Command

A valuable Excel Edit menu command is Undo. Any time you ask Excel to take an action, you often can immediately reverse the effects of the action by using the Undo command.

For example, suppose you wanted to reverse the effects of the previous Delete command on the credit card worksheet. Can Excel undo the delete operation and restore the original worksheet? Choose Undo Delete on the Edit menu.

Undo Delete command

When you choose Undo, Excel takes the following two actions:

1. Moves the information shown in column D to column E.
2. Retrieves the deleted column D information from memory and puts it back in column D.

	A	B	C	D	E	F	G	H
1	The Cost of Credit Card Procrastination							
2								
3	Annual interest rate (%)	12%	15%	18%	21%			
4	Monthly interest rate	0.01	0.0125	0.015	0.0175			
5	Monthly multiplier	1.01	1.0125	1.015	1.0175			
6	Original amount ($)	$1,000	$1,000	$1,000	$1,000			
7	After 1 month	$1,010	$1,013	$1,015	$1,018			
8	After 2 months	$1,020	$1,025	$1,030	$1,035			
9	After 3 months	$1,030	$1,038	$1,046	$1,053			
10	After 4 months	$1,041	$1,051	$1,061	$1,072			
11	After 5 months	$1,051	$1,064	$1,077	$1,091			
12	After 6 months	$1,062	$1,077	$1,093	$1,110			
13	After 7 months	$1,072	$1,091	$1,110	$1,129			
14	After 8 months	$1,083	$1,104	$1,126	$1,149			
15	After 9 months	$1,094	$1,118	$1,143	$1,169			
16	After 10 months	$1,105	$1,132	$1,161	$1,189			
17	After 11 months	$1,116	$1,146	$1,178	$1,210			
18	After 12 months	$1,127	$1,161	$1,196	$1,231			
19								
20								

Worksheet after the Undo command

As Excel moves cell information from column D back into column E, the program changes the cell references in the formulas to match the column E locations. The worksheet returns to the condition it was in before you used the Delete command.

The Insert Command

You can use the Edit menu's Insert command to insert a row or column of empty cells into a worksheet. Suppose you wanted to insert a column of empty cells between columns C and D on the credit card worksheet. First, you would select the cells in column D and then choose Insert on the Edit menu.

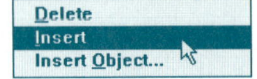

The Edit menu's Insert command

After you choose Insert, Excel does two things:

1. Moves all the cell information in columns D, E, and so on, one column position to the right. As the data are moved, Excel adjusts formula cell references to correspond to the data's new locations.
2. Clears the contents of all the cells in column D.

	A	B	C	D	E	F	G	H
1	The Cost of Credit Card Procrastination							
2								
3	Annual interest rate (%)	12%	15%		18%	21%		
4	Monthly interest rate	0.01	0.0125		0.015	0.0175		
5	Monthly multiplier	1.01	1.0125		1.015	1.0175		
6	Original amount ($)	$1,000	$1,000		$1,000	$1,000		
7	After 1 month	$1,010	$1,013		$1,015	$1,018		
8	After 2 months	$1,020	$1,025		$1,030	$1,035		
9	After 3 months	$1,030	$1,038		$1,046	$1,053		
10	After 4 months	$1,041	$1,051		$1,061	$1,072		
11	After 5 months	$1,051	$1,064		$1,077	$1,091		
12	After 6 months	$1,062	$1,077		$1,093	$1,110		
13	After 7 months	$1,072	$1,091		$1,110	$1,129		
14	After 8 months	$1,083	$1,104		$1,126	$1,149		
15	After 9 months	$1,094	$1,118		$1,143	$1,169		
16	After 10 months	$1,105	$1,132		$1,161	$1,189		
17	After 11 months	$1,116	$1,146		$1,178	$1,210		
18	After 12 months	$1,127	$1,161		$1,196	$1,231		
19								
20								

Worksheet after Insert command

If you wanted to use column D for another interest schedule calculation, you could copy the information from an adjacent column and paste that data into column D. But Excel provides a one-step method of performing this task as you insert a new column.

If you are following this example on your computer, choose Undo on the Edit menu to remove the column of empty cells that you just inserted. The worksheet returns to its original form.

Now select all the cells in column D (click the column D label), and choose the Copy command on the Edit menu. Excel will copy the column D cell information to the Clipboard. You will see the parade of "marching ants" surrounding the column D cells.

Open the Edit menu once again. You see an Insert Paste command on the menu immediately below the Delete command. The "Paste" part of the command indicates that you have something on the Clipboard.

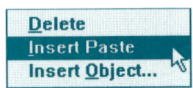

The Edit menu's Insert Paste command

Choose the Insert Paste command. Excel performs two actions:

1. Moves all the information in columns D, E, and so on, one column to the right. The program adjusts formula cell references to correspond to their new locations.

2. Clears the cells in column D and pastes the contents of the Clipboard into that column. If the contents of the pasted cells contain formulas, Excel adjusts cell references to match the new locations.

	A	B	C	D	E	F	G	H
1	The Cost of Credit Card Procrastination							
2								
3	Annual interest rate (%)	12%	15%	18%	18%	21%		
4	Monthly interest rate	0.01	0.0125	0.015	0.015	0.0175		
5	Monthly multiplier	1.01	1.0125	1.015	1.015	1.0175		
6	Original amount ($)	$1,000	$1,000	$1,000	$1,000	$1,000		
7	After 1 month	$1,010	$1,013	$1,015	$1,015	$1,018		
8	After 2 months	$1,020	$1,025	$1,030	$1,030	$1,035		
9	After 3 months	$1,030	$1,038	$1,046	$1,046	$1,053		
10	After 4 months	$1,041	$1,051	$1,061	$1,061	$1,072		
11	After 5 months	$1,051	$1,064	$1,077	$1,077	$1,091		
12	After 6 months	$1,062	$1,077	$1,093	$1,093	$1,110		
13	After 7 months	$1,072	$1,091	$1,110	$1,110	$1,129		
14	After 8 months	$1,083	$1,104	$1,126	$1,126	$1,149		
15	After 9 months	$1,094	$1,118	$1,143	$1,143	$1,169		
16	After 10 months	$1,105	$1,132	$1,161	$1,161	$1,189		
17	After 11 months	$1,116	$1,146	$1,178	$1,178	$1,210		
18	After 12 months	$1,127	$1,161	$1,196	$1,196	$1,231		
19								
20								

Worksheet after Insert Paste operation

You still see the "ants" marching around the borders of the column E cells. Click any worksheet cell to stop the parade.

Test the inserted formulas in column D by changing the annual percentage rate in cell D3. Select cell D3 (click the cell) and change the constant from 0.18 to 0.17. Type the value into the formula bar, with the decimal point, as in **.17**.

Click the enter box (the check mark icon) on the formula bar to store the new value and recalculate the worksheet. Once you enter this value, the format for cell D3 displays your entry of ".17" as 17%.

Chapter 5: Worksheet Magic

	A	B	C	D	E	F	G
	D3		0.17				
1	The Cost of Credit Card Procrastination						
2							
3	Annual interest rate (%)	12%	15%	17%	18%	21%	
4	Monthly interest rate	0.01	0.0125	0.014167	0.015	0.0175	
5	Monthly multiplier	1.01	1.0125	1.014167	1.015	1.0175	
6	Original amount ($)	$1,000	$1,000	$1,000	$1,000	$1,000	
7	After 1 month	$1,010	$1,013	$1,014	$1,015	$1,018	
8	After 2 months	$1,020	$1,025	$1,029	$1,030	$1,035	
9	After 3 months	$1,030	$1,038	$1,043	$1,046	$1,053	
10	After 4 months	$1,041	$1,051	$1,058	$1,061	$1,072	
11	After 5 months	$1,051	$1,064	$1,073	$1,077	$1,091	
12	After 6 months	$1,062	$1,077	$1,088	$1,093	$1,110	
13	After 7 months	$1,072	$1,091	$1,103	$1,110	$1,129	
14	After 8 months	$1,083	$1,104	$1,119	$1,126	$1,149	
15	After 9 months	$1,094	$1,118	$1,135	$1,143	$1,169	
16	After 10 months	$1,105	$1,132	$1,151	$1,161	$1,189	
17	After 11 months	$1,116	$1,146	$1,167	$1,178	$1,210	
18	After 12 months	$1,127	$1,161	$1,184	$1,196	$1,231	
19							
20							

Worksheet with new value in cell D3

Excel recalculates results using the new value in cell D3. Examine the data in column D. They look reasonable when compared to the interest schedule data in columns C and E. The inserted formulas appear to be working as expected.

Let Excel Find the Cells

As you enter data and formulas, and format worksheet cells, Excel records the information for each cell. The program uses that information to help refresh the screen display and to perform and check calculations.

Excel has a handy tool, the Select Special command on the Formula menu, that lets you select all cells that have the same type of contents. For example, you can ask Excel to select all cells containing only text constants, or all cells with formulas, or all the blank cells within a specified range.

To see how this tool performs, let's continue to use the credit card worksheet with the newly

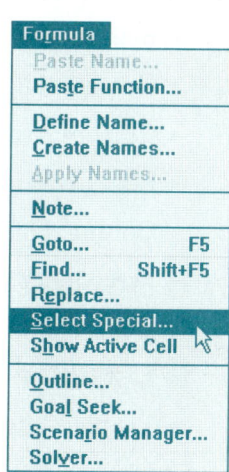

The Formula menu's Select Special command

88 Simply Excel

inserted column D. Open the Formula menu and choose the Select Special command.

The Select Special dialog box appears.

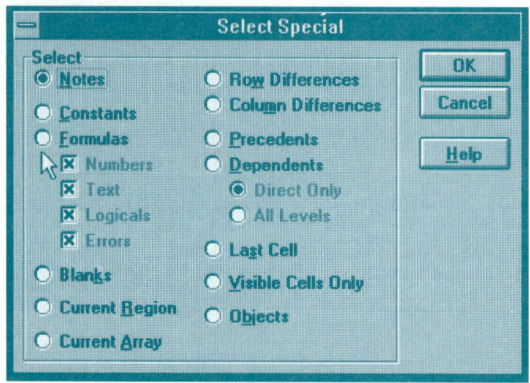

Select Special dialog box

The circular option buttons near the center and on the left side of the dialog box refer to the 13 types of cell contents that can be isolated with this tool. Those content types are:

- Notes
- Constants
- Formulas
- Blanks
- Current Region
- Current Array
- Row Differences
- Column Differences
- Precedents
- Dependents
- Last Cell
- Visible Cells Only
- Objects

Chapter 5: Worksheet Magic   **89**

To continue exploring how this feature works, click the Constants button on the dialog box.

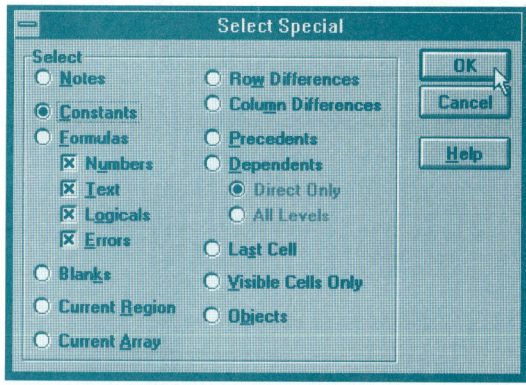

Constants option selected

When you click Constants, you activate the sub-option check boxes: Numbers, Text, Logicals, and Errors. The X's in the boxes indicate that these options are selected or turned on. For now, leave those sub-options on and click OK. The combination of settings you have made tells Excel to select all worksheet cells that contain any type of constant.

	A	B	C	D	E	F	G	H
1	The Cost of Credit Card Procrastination							
2								
3	Annual interest rate (%)	12%	15%	17%	18%	21%		
4	Monthly interest rate	0.01	0.0125	0.014167	0.015	0.0175		
5	Monthly multiplier	1.01	1.0125	1.014167	1.015	1.0175		
6	Original amount ($)	$1,000	$1,000	$1,000	$1,000	$1,000		
7	After 1 month	$1,010	$1,013	$1,014	$1,015	$1,018		
8	After 2 months	$1,020	$1,025	$1,029	$1,030	$1,035		
9	After 3 months	$1,030	$1,038	$1,043	$1,046	$1,053		
10	After 4 months	$1,041	$1,051	$1,058	$1,061	$1,072		
11	After 5 months	$1,051	$1,064	$1,073	$1,077	$1,091		
12	After 6 months	$1,062	$1,077	$1,088	$1,093	$1,110		
13	After 7 months	$1,072	$1,091	$1,103	$1,110	$1,129		
14	After 8 months	$1,083	$1,104	$1,119	$1,126	$1,149		
15	After 9 months	$1,094	$1,118	$1,135	$1,143	$1,169		
16	After 10 months	$1,105	$1,132	$1,151	$1,161	$1,189		
17	After 11 months	$1,116	$1,146	$1,167	$1,178	$1,210		
18	After 12 months	$1,127	$1,161	$1,184	$1,196	$1,231		
19								
20								

Only cells with constants selected

Excel selects cell A1, cells A3 through A18, cells B3 through F3, and cell B6. Each of these cells contains either a text or a numeric constant.

The type of selection that Excel has made is called a *nonadjacent selection* of cells. Excel does not confine cell selection just to single cells or to cells that are next to each other.

What if you only wanted to look at the cells with numeric constants? Choose Select Special on the Formula menu.

When the Select Special dialog box appears, click the Constants button. Then click the Text check box to turn off that option. When you have made these two choices, click OK.

	A	B	C	D	E	F	G
1	The Cost of Credit Card Procrastination						
2							
3	Annual interest rate (%)	12%	15%	17%	18%	21%	
4	Monthly interest rate	0.01	0.0125	0.014167	0.015	0.0175	
5	Monthly multiplier	1.01	1.0125	1.014167	1.015	1.0175	
6	Original amount ($)	$1,000	$1,000	$1,000	$1,000	$1,000	
7	After 1 month	$1,010	$1,013	$1,014	$1,015	$1,018	
8	After 2 months	$1,020	$1,025	$1,029	$1,030	$1,035	
9	After 3 months	$1,030	$1,038	$1,043	$1,046	$1,053	
10	After 4 months	$1,041	$1,051	$1,058	$1,061	$1,072	
11	After 5 months	$1,051	$1,064	$1,073	$1,077	$1,091	
12	After 6 months	$1,062	$1,077	$1,088	$1,093	$1,110	
13	After 7 months	$1,072	$1,091	$1,103	$1,110	$1,129	
14	After 8 months	$1,083	$1,104	$1,119	$1,126	$1,149	
15	After 9 months	$1,094	$1,118	$1,135	$1,143	$1,169	
16	After 10 months	$1,105	$1,132	$1,151	$1,161	$1,189	
17	After 11 months	$1,116	$1,146	$1,167	$1,178	$1,210	
18	After 12 months	$1,127	$1,161	$1,184	$1,196	$1,231	
19							
20							

Only cells with numeric constants selected

Excel selects cells B3 through F3, and cell B6. These are the six worksheet cells with numeric constants.

Some of the advantages of making this type of nonadjacent selection include being able to:

- Clear the selected cells with one use of the Edit menu's Clear command.

- Move around the selected cells using the TAB and SHIFT-TAB keys on the keyboard.

- Locate specific cells and types of cells when you are troubleshooting worksheet problems.

For this particular example, being able to locate and move around just the cells containing the numeric constants provides a handy way to alter the constants for "what-if" scenarios.

If you are following along on your computer, try this: Use the TAB and SHIFT-TAB keys to move around the selected cells. If you continue to press TAB, the highlight moves across the screen from cell B3, to C3, D3, E3, and F3. It then jumps to cell B6, and then back up to B3. If you press and hold down SHIFT-TAB, the highlight travels in the opposite direction.

What if you wanted to select all the cells with formulas? Before you can use the Select Special tool to identify those cells, you have to click a cell on the worksheet to release the current selection. This selection contains only cells with numeric constants; there are no cells in this group with formulas. If you tried a search for formulas within the current selection, you would receive the message "No cells found."

Click cell D3 to release the current selection. Then choose Select Special on the Formula menu. When the Select Special dialog box appears, click Formulas.

Click OK to tell Excel to select all the cells that contain formulas. A nonadjacent selection of cells with formulas will appear on the screen.

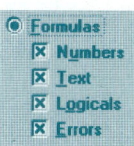

Selecting cells with formulas

	A	B	C	D	E	F	G	H
1	The Cost of Credit Card Procrastination							
2								
3	Annual interest rate (%)	12%	15%	17%	18%	21%		
4	Monthly interest rate	0.01	0.0125	0.014167	0.015	0.0175		
5	Monthly multiplier	1.01	1.0125	1.014167	1.015	1.0175		
6	Original amount ($)	$1,000	$1,000	$1,000	$1,000	$1,000		
7	After 1 month	$1,010	$1,013	$1,014	$1,015	$1,018		
8	After 2 months	$1,020	$1,025	$1,029	$1,030	$1,035		
9	After 3 months	$1,030	$1,038	$1,043	$1,046	$1,053		
10	After 4 months	$1,041	$1,051	$1,058	$1,061	$1,072		
11	After 5 months	$1,051	$1,064	$1,073	$1,077	$1,091		
12	After 6 months	$1,062	$1,077	$1,088	$1,093	$1,110		
13	After 7 months	$1,072	$1,091	$1,103	$1,110	$1,129		
14	After 8 months	$1,083	$1,104	$1,119	$1,126	$1,149		
15	After 9 months	$1,094	$1,118	$1,135	$1,143	$1,169		
16	After 10 months	$1,105	$1,132	$1,151	$1,161	$1,189		
17	After 11 months	$1,116	$1,146	$1,167	$1,178	$1,210		
18	After 12 months	$1,127	$1,161	$1,184	$1,196	$1,231		
19								
20								

Cell reference: C4 = C3/12

Only cells with formulas selected

The selection is nonadjacent since there are actually three regions highlighted. Cell B6 contains a constant and is not part of the selection. The active cell, C4, is selected and does not show a highlight.

If you are following along on your computer, use the TAB and SHIFT-TAB keys to move around the selected cells. If you press and hold down the TAB key, the highlight zooms from cell C4 down to cell F6, jumps to cells B4 and B5, and then jumps to B7 and travels down to cell F18. Each cell you traverse displays a formula in the formula bar.

If you wish, continue to explore the Select Special tool's options on your own. This worksheet has no notes or graphic objects. It does contain a few blank cells and a last cell; all of its cells are visible.

Experiment with the Precedents and Dependents options. These options show you how cells are connected by formulas. They provide a way of tracing backward (precedent) and forward (dependent) through Excel's calculations. They are like an electronic version of "the knee bone is connected to the ankle bone" for worksheet formulas and calculations

Let Excel Do the Work

In the last section, you learned that Excel can help you locate cells containing specific types of information. Excel can also help you generate worksheet data entries. It does so by looking at the first few data items and making an educated guess as to what the rest should be.

Sound like magic? Not really. What Excel does is follow a few simple, logical rules. The results just look magical.

The Fill Feature

Starting with a blank worksheet, put a single numeric constant, like 100, in cell B3.

Chapter 5: Worksheet Magic

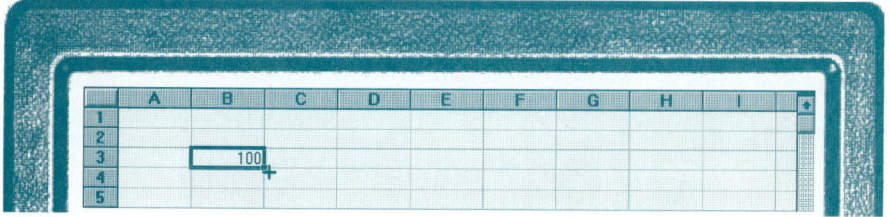

Blank worksheet with numeric constant

After you enter 100 into cell B3, the cell is the active cell and is enclosed in a selection rectangle. In the lower-right corner of the selection is a small, solid square, called the *fill handle*. This is one of two Excel tools that help you create data entries. The second tool is the Series command on the Data menu.

Let's examine the fill handle first. Position the mouse pointer over the fill handle. The pointer changes from either an arrow or a "fat" Plus sign icon to a "thin" Plus sign icon.

Use the pointer to click and drag the fill handle across the screen to cell H3. When you release the mouse button, you see seven cells (B3 through H3) filled with the value 100.

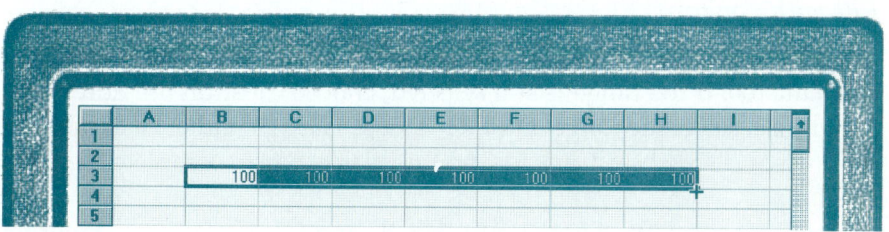

Result of dragging the fill handle on the active cell

When you click and drag the fill handle of an active cell, Excel automatically copies the contents of the cell (either a constant or a formula) into the selected adjacent cells. Excel does not restrict this operation to a single cell; it can be performed with a range of cells.

For example, click the fill handle (lower-right corner of cell H3) for the selected range of cells, and drag the handle down the screen to H14. Now you see 84 cells (12 rows by 7 columns) filled with the constant 100.

Filling down the screen

Excel can perform this feat with both text and numeric constants. You can also use the Fill Right and Fill Down commands on the Edit menu to accomplish the same thing.

Fill with Gusto

Clear the entire data range (B3 through H14) that has been filled with the constant 100. If the range is still selected, choose Clear on the Edit menu. Otherwise, select the range and then choose Clear. In either case, you will see a Clear dialog box. Click OK on this dialog box to complete the Clear operation.

Enter the constants 1 and 2 into cells B3 and C3, respectively. Enter the constants 1 and 3 into cells B4 and C4, respectively. After you enter these last two constants, select all four cells.

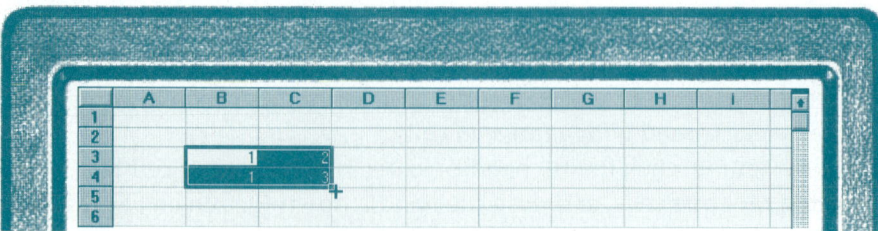

Four constants entered

Click and drag the fill handle to the right, to cell H4. What happened? Can you guess?

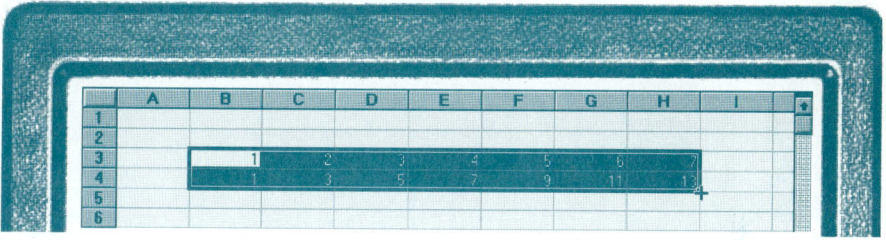

Excel creates two series of data entries

Excel looked at the first two data entries on each row and made an intelligent guess for the remaining entries. Seeing 1 and 2 on row 3, Excel assumed that the remaining row 3 entries should be 4, 5, 6, 7. That is, the program assumed that you intended to create a series of constants that increased by a value of 1.

In row 4, Excel looked at the first two entries (1 and 3), and assumed that you wanted a series that varied by a value of 2. The program produced 5, 7, 9, 11, and 13 to fill out row 4.

What other feats can Excel perform? Try this. Clear the worksheet and enter the following constants into the indicated cells:

Cell	Constant
B3	January
B4	Mon
B5	12/30/93
B6	11 pm
B7	Qtr 1
B8	Item 1
B9	100

After you enter the constants, select the cells and click the center alignment icon on the toolbar. This will align the entries in the center of the cells, and produce a selection rectangle and fill handle for the next experiment.

Constants entered and aligned

Click and drag the fill handle to column H (cell H9). Amazing results! Excel recognizes certain types of constants (months, days, dates, and times) and creates appropriate data series from single data values.

Excel creates several data series

Excel recognized the month entry (row 3) and created six more month names, in order, to fill out that series. In row 4, the program recognized the abbreviated name for a day (Mon) and filled out a week's worth of names, all shortened appropriately.

Row 5 is quite interesting. Excel recognized data in a month/day/year format (12/30/93) and added six more dates to that row. When the dates crossed into a new year, Excel updated both the month and year parts of the entries. It might be fun to see what Excel does at the end of February in a leap year.

In row 6, Excel extended the time across the midnight hour. The program changes PM to AM when the clock strikes twelve. Also, did you notice that when the data (11 pm) was entered in cell B6, Excel automatically formatted the entry as 11:00 PM?

"Qtr" is another type of date entry that Excel understands. Excel expects financial worksheets to use dates in all forms (years, quarters, months, weeks, days). The program was designed to handle all types of date entries appropriately. In this case, Excel knows that "Qtr" stands for Quarter and extends the series, changing back to Qtr 1 (cell F7) after Qtr 4 (cell E7).

The entry in cell B8, "Item 1," is not a date entry. However, Excel evaluates every constant during a fill operation, even text constants, and looks for entries that can be extended into a series. The numeric part of this text constant can be extended into a series, and Excel does so automatically.

What about the final entry, 100 (in cell B9)? Under regular fill conditions, Excel would simply reproduce this constant in the six remaining cells. However, since the range of cells being extended included entries that were being incremented, Excel assumed that the constant in cell B9 should be incremented as well.

The Series Command

For the data entries used in the previous examples (cells B3 through B9), the Data menu's Series command, and the AutoFill option that appears on that command's dialog box, create the same results you produced with the fill handle. If you can do so, try the Series command and the AutoFill option, and verify that you get identical results.

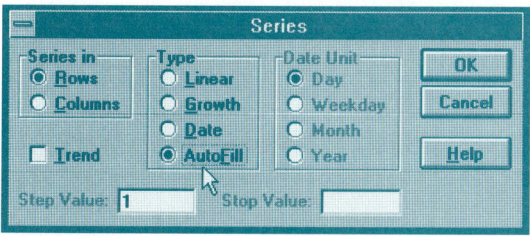

The Series dialog box

You can use the fill handle to generate all but a few types of series data. The few that you cannot create with the fill handle—namely, a few series that deal with trends and forecasts—you can create using the Series command's Trend option. You will learn more about the Series command and the Trend option later in this book.

You have completed your second exploration of Excel's worksheet features. Next, you will revisit Excel's chart tool and discover more of Excel's "magic."

Chart Power

6

In Chapter 3, you became acquainted with the Excel ChartWizard. You used the ChartWizard to transform a range of worksheet data into many different chart formats.

In this chapter, you will explore a few of Excel's chart editing features, as well as the program's amazing drawing and slide show capabilities.

Excel Chart Editing Features

In Chapter 3, you created a 3-D column chart based on a set of estimated revenues for multimedia products and services. When you recreate that same chart with ChartWizard, you see the following initial display:

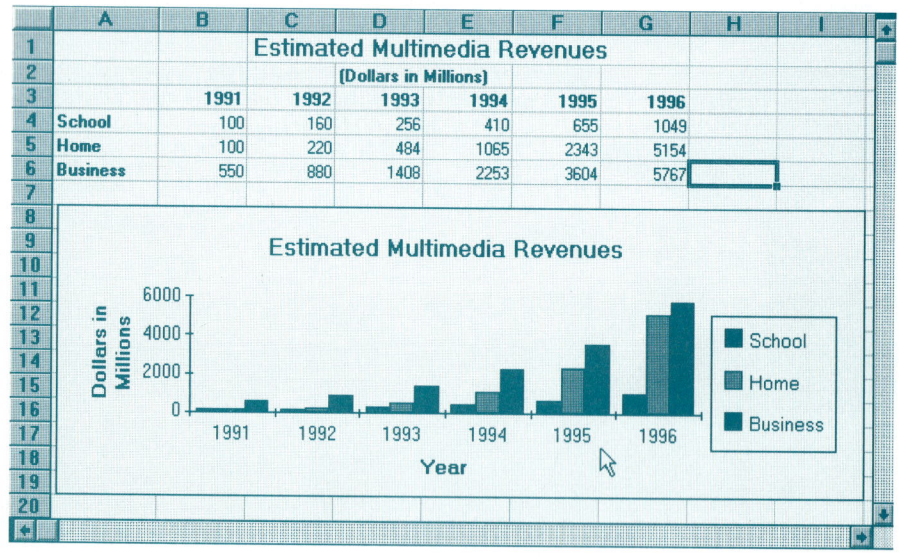

Multimedia Revenues worksheet

Double-clicking on the chart expands it to fill the window. The chart toolbar appears at the bottom of the screen.

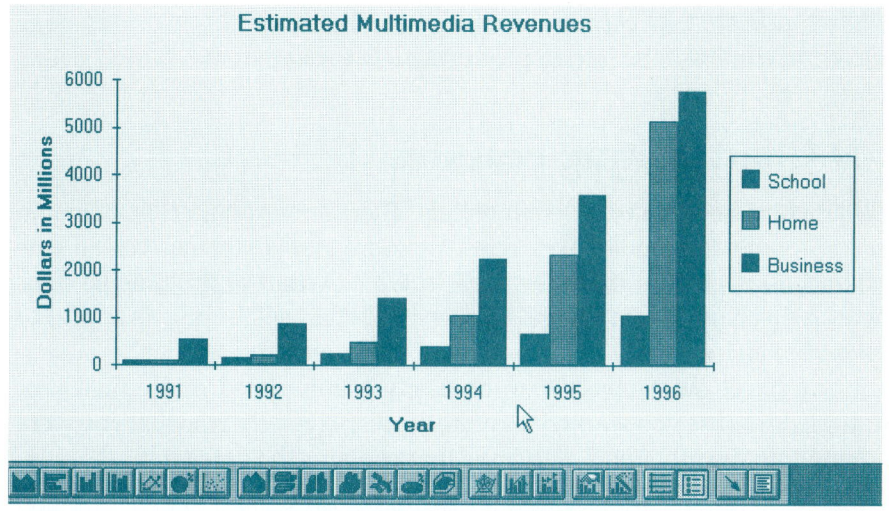

Chart expanded into a window

For this set of 3-D activities, the legend tool (the third icon from the right end of the toolbar) has been clicked to hide the legend.

The Legend tool

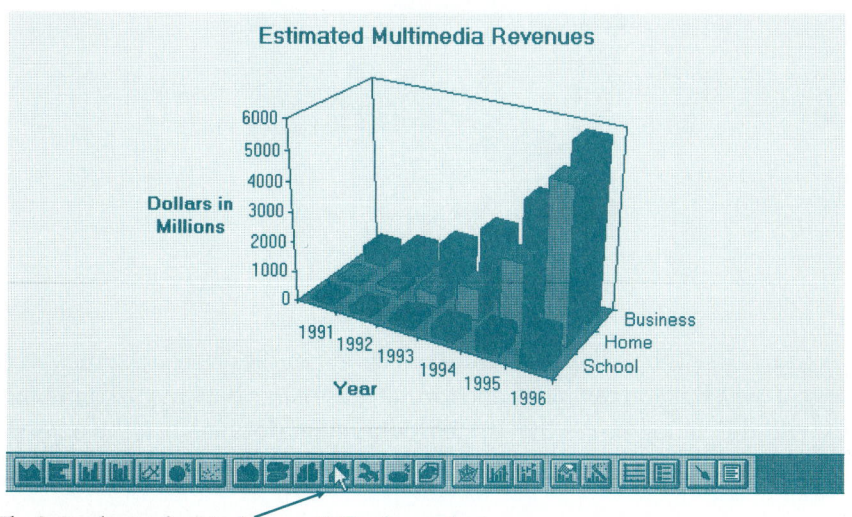

The 3-D column chart tool   3-D column chart

Next, use the 3-D column chart tool as shown on the previous page (eleventh icon from the left) to produce a 3-D version of the charted data.

3-D Chart Editing Features

A chart consists of many different objects. There are text objects that contain the text for the chart and its axes' titles. There are the axes themselves, and the text and numbers that mark the axes. In the 3-D chart of multimedia data, there are 18 colorful data columns. For the 3-D chart, all the objects appear to rest within an imaginary "box," with two "rear walls" and a "floor."

Many Excel chart objects can be easily manipulated and edited. For example, suppose you wanted to rotate the displayed chart so that you were looking into the other end of the box that contains the data.

If you click one of the rear walls of the box, you will see a set of white selection handles. The chart's two rear walls are really a single graphic object; you have just selected that object.

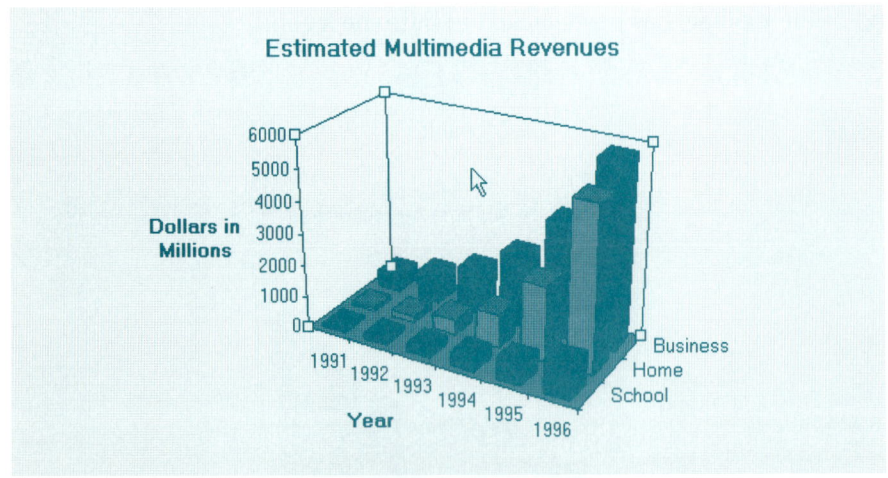

Chart object with white selection handles

A chart object that displays white selection handles cannot be moved or sized directly. But you can move and format these items with menu commands and with the dialog boxes that appear when you double-click the objects.

If you click a corner of the box, a set of black selection handles appears. In this case, you have selected the chart itself as a single object. Chart objects marked with black selection handles can be moved and sized with the mouse, directly on the screen.

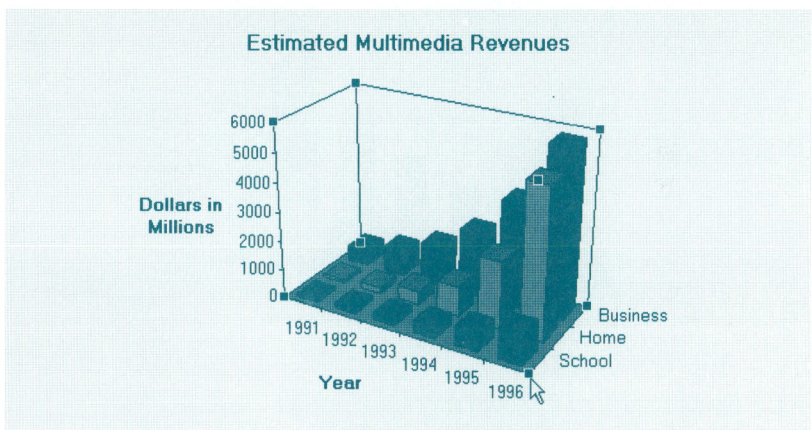

Chart object with black selection handles

To see how this feature works, click the black selection handle on the near, front corner, and hold down the mouse button. A wireframe image of the 3-D chart replaces the chart itself. The wireframe outlines the edges of the chart, and marks the positions of the three data columns.

Now, drag the mouse to the right. The wireframe rotates into a new position as you move the mouse pointer.

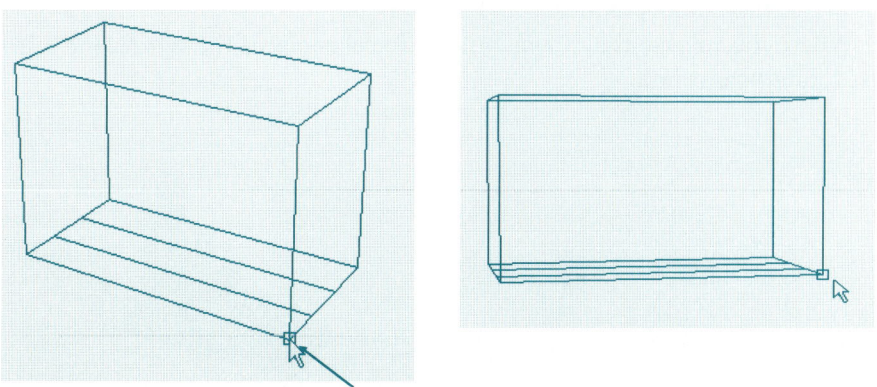

Chart wireframe image *Click here and drag to the right* *Wireframe rotated to the right*

After you rotate the wireframe to the right as far as it will go, release the mouse button. Another amazing Excel feat! Excel has rotated the entire chart to match the last position of the wireframe.

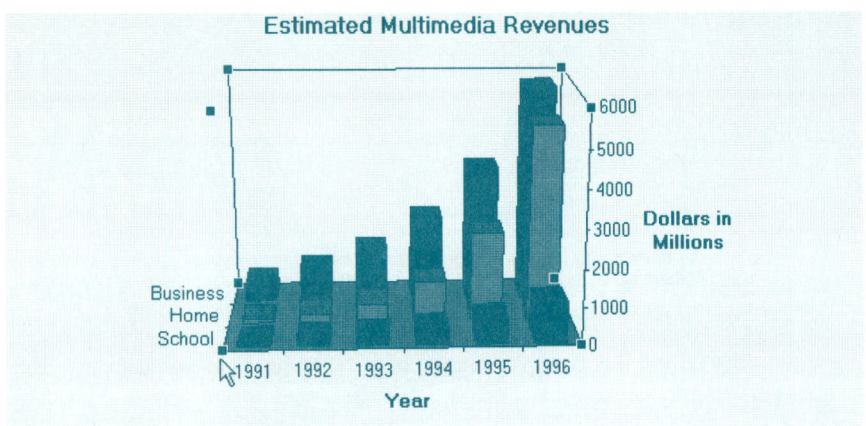

3-D chart after initial rotation

In rotating the chart, Excel made a few automatic adjustments. The program moved all the axes' labels to correspond to the chart's new orientation. (The value axis was switched from the left to the right side, and the categories Business, Home, and School were switched to the left side.) It also removed the "wall" that was on the left side of the box, and put a new "wall" on the right side.

To continue the chart's rotation, click and drag the handle on the left front corner to the right. As you move the mouse to the right, the wireframe revolves into a new position.

When you release the mouse button, Excel replaces the wireframe with the rotated chart image.

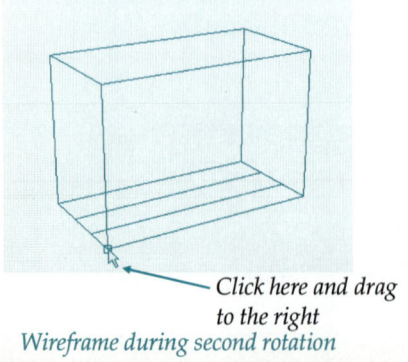

Click here and drag to the right

Wireframe during second rotation   *Final 3-d chart*

If you have this chart on your computer, try other experiments with Excel's 3-D editing features. Rotate the chart until you are looking down into the box. Shift the chart around until you are looking up through the bottom of the box.

Another Way to Edit 3-D Charts

Excel also provides a command on the Format menu, 3-D View, that allows you to edit and move 3-D charts with a dialog box. Use the 3-D View command when you need more precise control over a chart's movement and positioning.

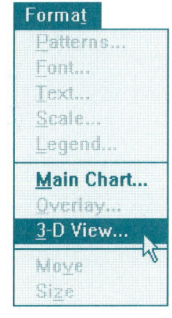

3-D View command on Format menu

Column Chart Editing Features

Let's look at another chart editing feature. Click the column chart tool (third icon from the left) on the chart toolbar. Excel displays the data as a two-dimensional column chart.

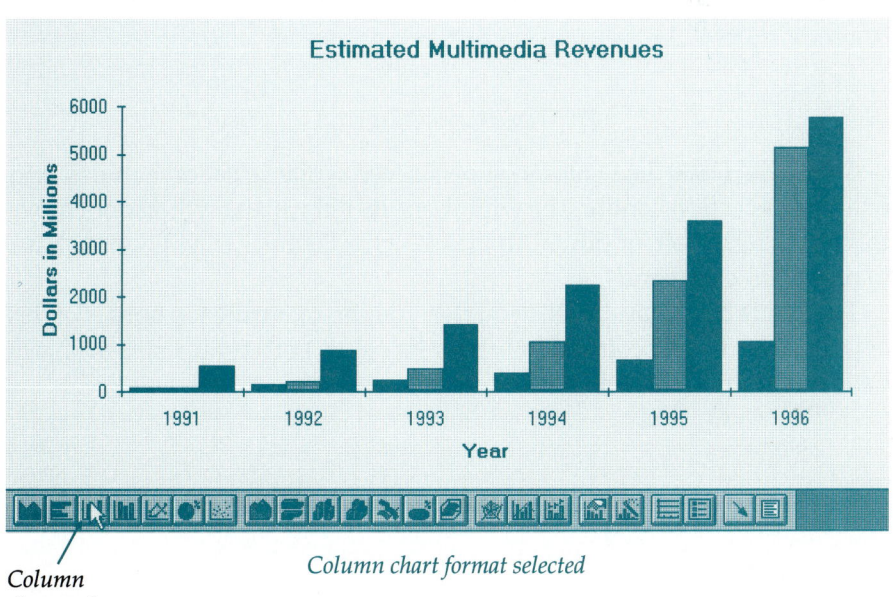

Column chart tool

Column chart format selected

Also, click the legend tool (third icon from the right end of the chart toolbar) to show the legend once again.

On an Excel column chart, each data column is a separate object. For example, hold down the CTRL key and click the Home data column for 1995 (the middle column). Several selection handles appear. (Note: On a Macintosh computer, you hold down the Command key and click the chart object to make this selection.)

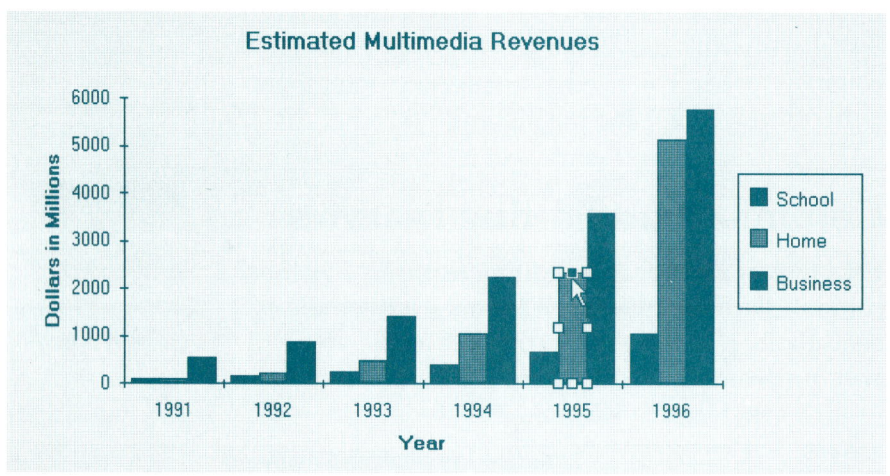

1995 Home Revenues selected

The 1995 Home data column shows seven white selection handles, and one black selection handle. The white handles tell you that you cannot move this object right, left, or down. To make such adjustments, you would have to use menu commands.

The single black handle tells you that you can move the top border of this object upwards, and concurrently alter its value. Let's try it. Click the black handle and drag it up the screen.

Chapter 6: Chart Power 109

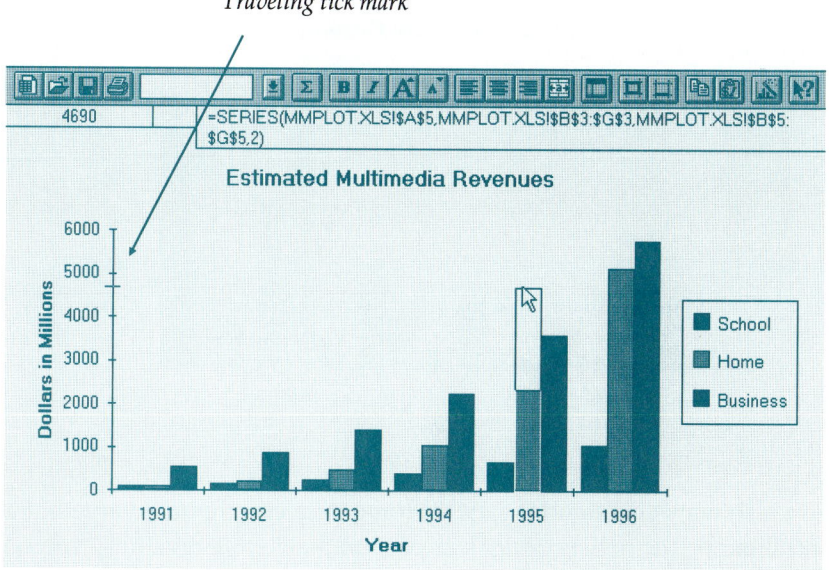

1995 Home Revenues being adjusted to 5000

A wireframe the width of the data column appears and moves up the screen. On the Y-axis, you see a traveling tick mark that moves as you move the mouse and the wireframe. The tick mark tells you the current position of the top of the data column. In the formula bar, Excel displays the value that corresponds to the mark's position on the axis.

For example, suppose you are in the middle of a presentation and someone mentions a new multimedia product. The product will come to market in 1995, and will revolutionize how people use video and audio in the home. The product will greatly affect the Home revenues in both 1995 and 1996.

To demonstrate the effect of the new product, you want to adjust the 1995 Home data column to show a value of 5000. Normally, you would go back to the worksheet and enter the new data there. But, for discussion purposes, you decide to adjust the chart directly.

You click and drag the black handle on the top of that column upwards until the value in the formula bar shows 5000. At this point, you can release the mouse button to view the adjusted chart column.

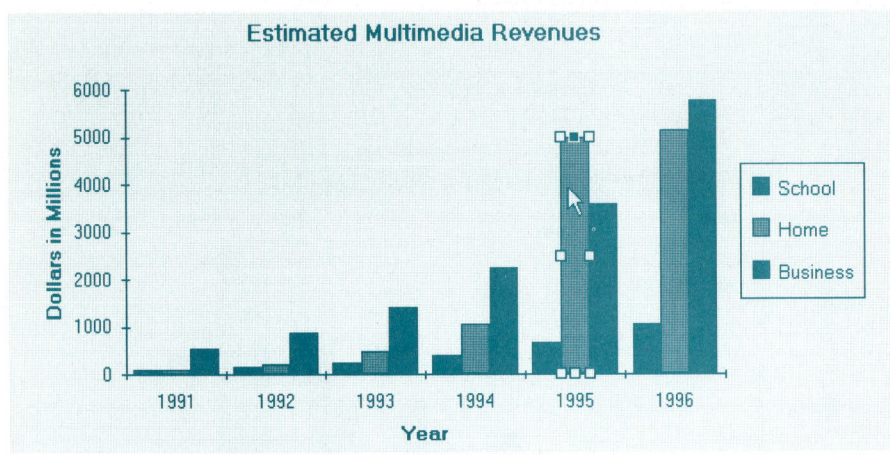

1995 Home Revenues adjusted to 5000

You also want to extend the 1996 Home data column to a value of 6000 to demonstrate the new product's impact on that year's revenues. You hold down CTRL (or Command on the Macintosh) and click the 1996 Home data column. The selection rectangles appear.

You then click and drag the black handle on this column up the screen until it reaches a value of 6000. When you release the mouse button, the adjusted data column appears on the chart.

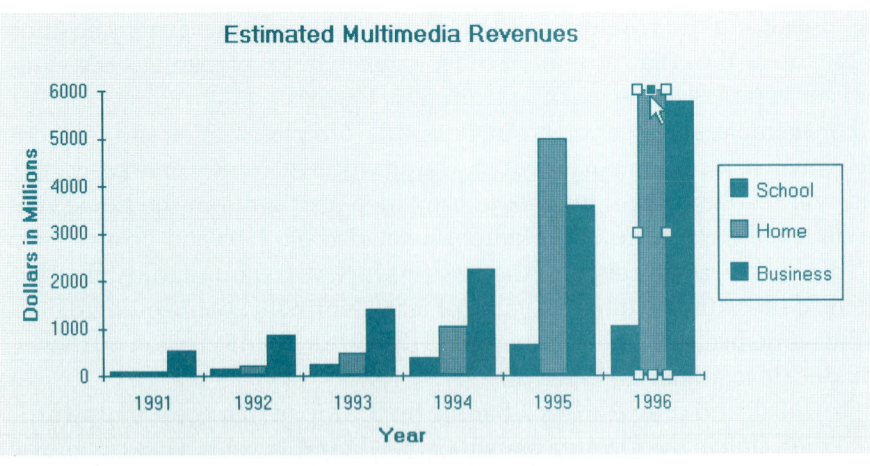

1996 Home Revenues adjusted to 6000

Switch back to the worksheet display using the Window menu. Excel has retained the changes you made to the chart columns, and shows those adjusted columns on the display. But look at the 1995 and 1996 Home data values.

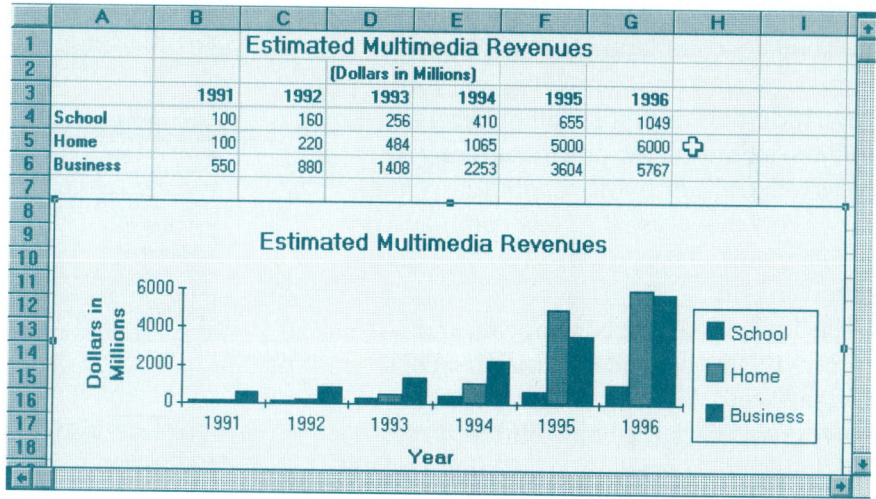

Chart adjustments reflected by worksheet data

Excel updated the worksheet data based on the adjustments made to the chart. You created the chart from the data in the worksheet cells, and Excel recorded the linkages involved. So, if you change the chart, Excel adjusts the worksheet data automatically.

In Excel, you can edit any attribute of an object on a chart. You can change the font and style of text in text boxes. You can specify an object's colors and patterns. You can move objects, and control their positions and orientations.

To make these changes, you first select a chart object by holding down the CTRL key and clicking the object. (On the Macintosh, hold down the Command key and click the object.) Two or more selection handles will appear on the object. If the selected object has black handles, you can move, resize, and change the object directly with the mouse.

If the handles are white, double-click the object. This action opens a dialog box that lets you change some of the object's attributes. You can also use commands on the Edit, Gallery, Chart, and Format menus to edit and change an object's attributes.

The Excel Drawing Tools

You have seen two of Excel's nine toolbars: the standard toolbar and the chart toolbar. The Toolbars command on the Options menu displays a dialog box that lets you show, hide, and customize all of Excel's toolbars, including the one that gives you access to Excel's drawing capabilities. Open a new worksheet (use the New command on the File menu). Then, choose Toolbars on the Options menu.

The Toolbars dialog box appears and displays the list of available toolbars. Let's explore Excel's drawing features. Select Drawing and click the Show button.

A dialog box appears that contains a set of Excel drawing tool icons. Excel toolbars can be displayed in two ways: in a floating dialog box form (as here) or as a bar of icons.

To display the drawing tools in the form of a bar of icons, double-click the title bar of the Drawing dialog box. The floating dialog box closes, and the drawing toolbar appears between the standard toolbar and the formula bar at the top of the screen.

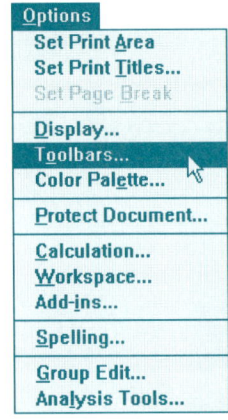

Toolbars command on the Options menu

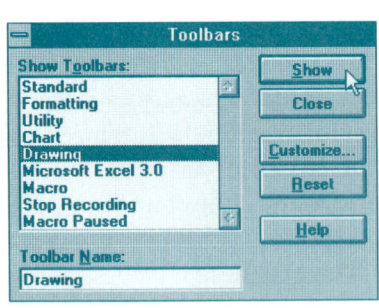

Toolbars dialog box

Double-click here to change to bar format

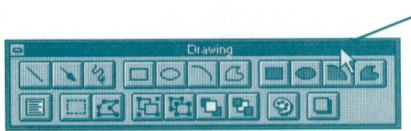

Drawing toolbar in dialog box format

Chapter 6: Chart Power   **113**

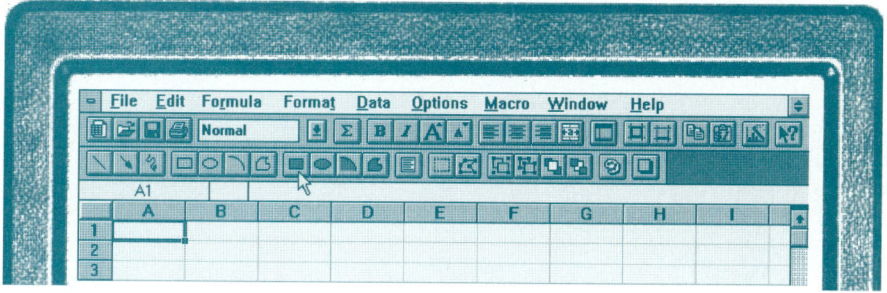

Drawing oolbar in bar format

The drawing toolbar displays 20 icons. Starting on the left, the icons represent the following Excel drawing tools:

1. Line tool
2. Arrow tool
3. Freehand tool
4. Rectangle tool
5. Oval tool
6. Arc tool
7. Freehand Polygon tool
8. Filled Rectangle tool
9. Filled Oval tool
10. Filled Arc tool
11. Filled Freehand Polygon tool
12. Text Box tool
13. Selection tool
14. Reshape tool
15. Group tool
16. Ungroup tool
17. Send to Front tool
18. Send to Back tool
19. Color tool
20. Drop Shadow tool

Create Graphics on the Worksheet

Let's try one of these tools. Click the Filled Rectangle tool (eighth icon from the left end of the toolbar). Move the mouse pointer onto the worksheet. The pointer turns into a small cross.

Click and drag the pointer to define a rectangular shape on the worksheet. In the following illustration, the pointer was clicked and dragged from a point in cell A2 to a point in cell D12.

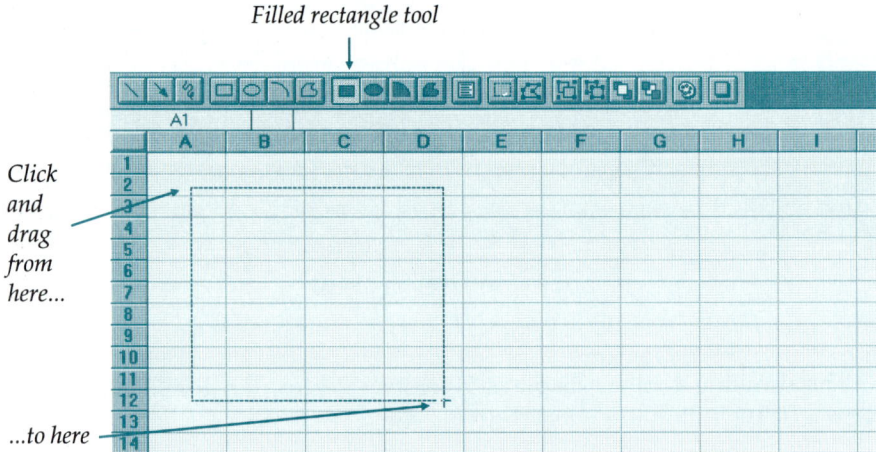

Filled rectangle tool in use

When you release the mouse button, a filled, white rectangle appears on the screen, marked with black selection handles.

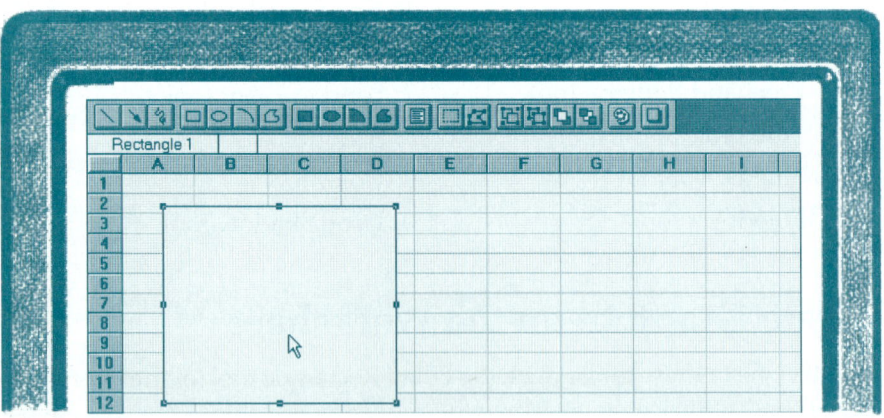

Filled rectangle object drawn on worksheet

The color tool (second icon from the right end of the toolbar) lets you easily alter the color of a selected graphic object. Each time you click the tool, the color of the selected object changes. Click the color tool several times and watch as the rectangle cycles through a rainbow of brilliant colors.

Chapter 6: Chart Power   **115**

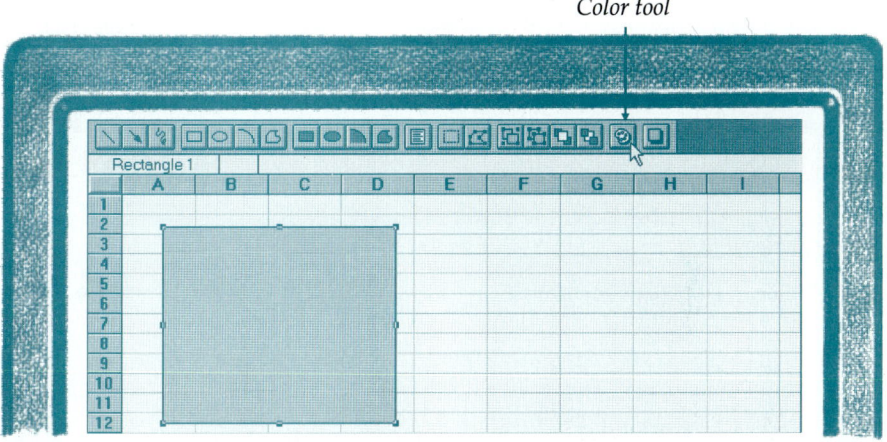

Chart color tool changes colors of rectangle

Click the Filled Oval tool (one icon to the right of the Filled Rectangle tool). Click and drag the mouse pointer to draw a circle on top of the rectangle.

If you are following this example on your computer, the position and size of the graphic objects are not really important for this activity. Simply draw the objects and position them roughly as shown in the illustrations.

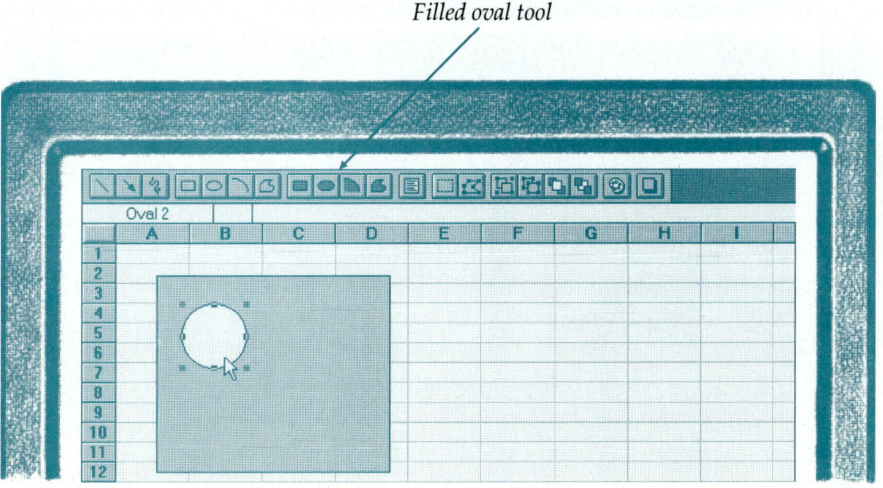

Circular object drawn with Filled oval tool

Use the color tool to change the color of the selected circle to red.

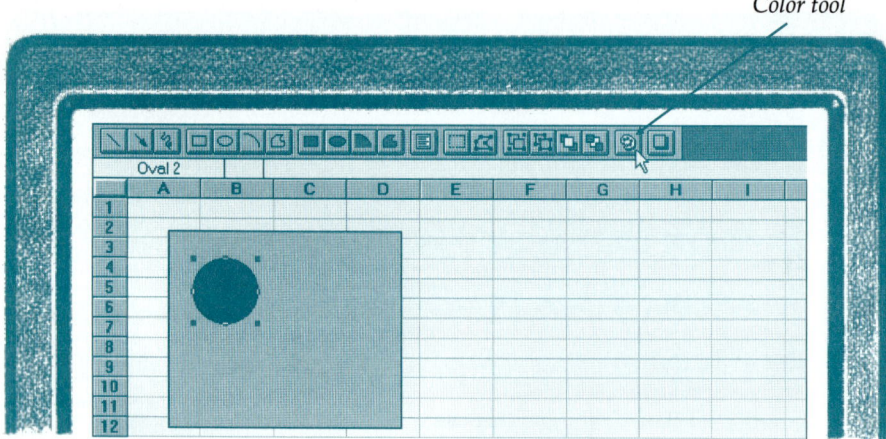

Color of circular object changed to red

Using the text box tool (ninth icon from the right end of the toolbar), click and drag to put a text box on the drawing. Draw the text box over the lower-right part of the rectangle.

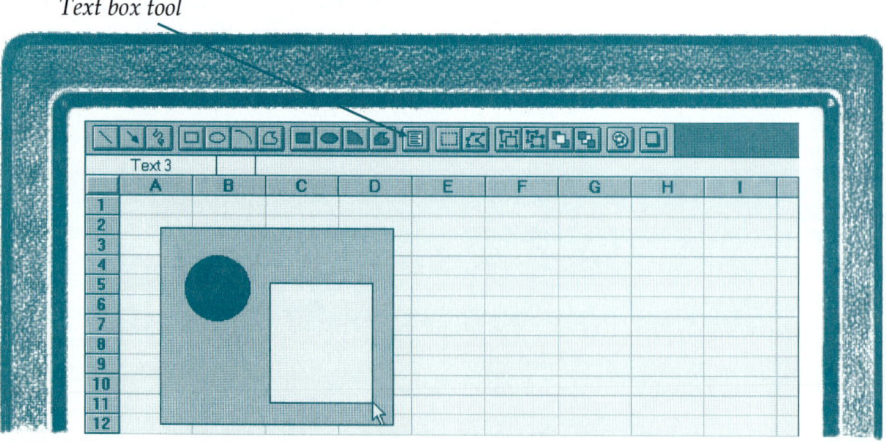

Text box object drawn on worksheet

Chapter 6: Chart Power   **117**

Click the selection tool (one icon to the right of the text box tool). Move the mouse pointer to cell A2 just outside the upper-left corner of the rectangle. Click and drag the pointer to cell D13 and release the mouse button.

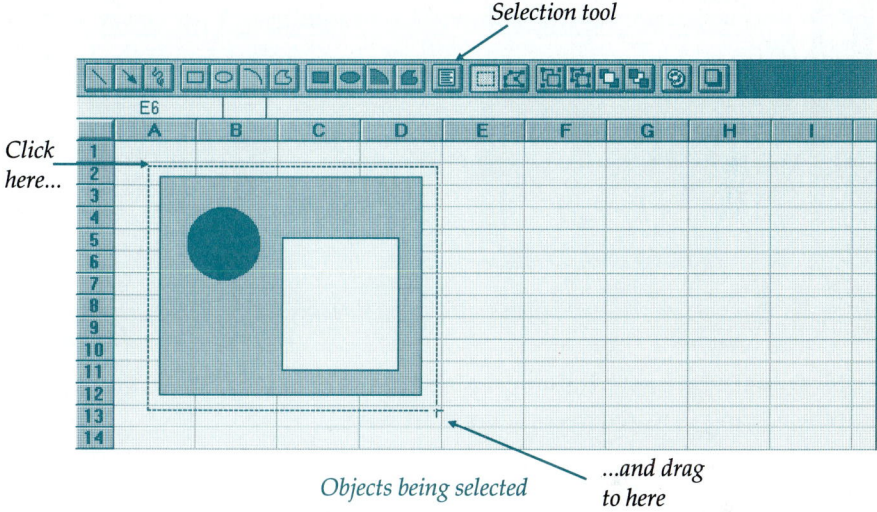

Objects being selected   *...and drag to here*

When you release the mouse button, selection handles appear on all three objects. They have been selected as a group.

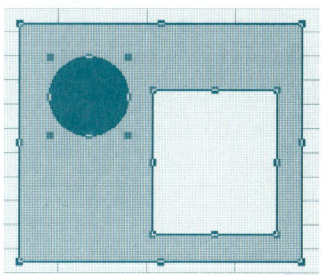

Objects selected as a group

Click the Drop Shadow tool at the right end of the drawing toolbar. Shadows appear at the right side and bottom of all three selected objects.

118   Simply Excel

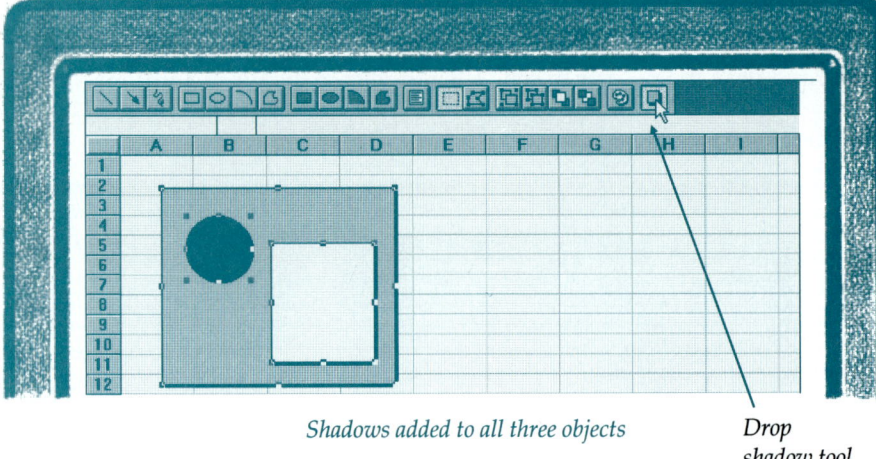

Shadows added to all three objects   *Drop shadow tool*

Now that you have drawn graphic objects on a worksheet, you can use Excel's editing features to copy your art work.

Copy and Paste Excel Graphics

With the three graphic objects selected as a group, choose the Copy command on the Edit menu.

Excel puts a copy of the objects on the Clipboard. Select cell E2 to the right of the three original objects. Selecting this cell will give Excel a "target," upper-left corner location for the upcoming paste operation.

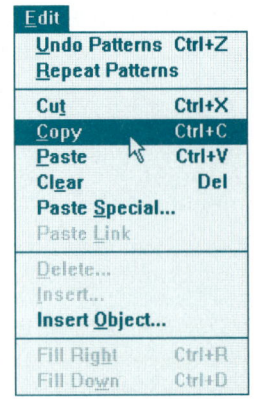

Selected ogjects being copied

Chapter 6: Chart Power   **119**

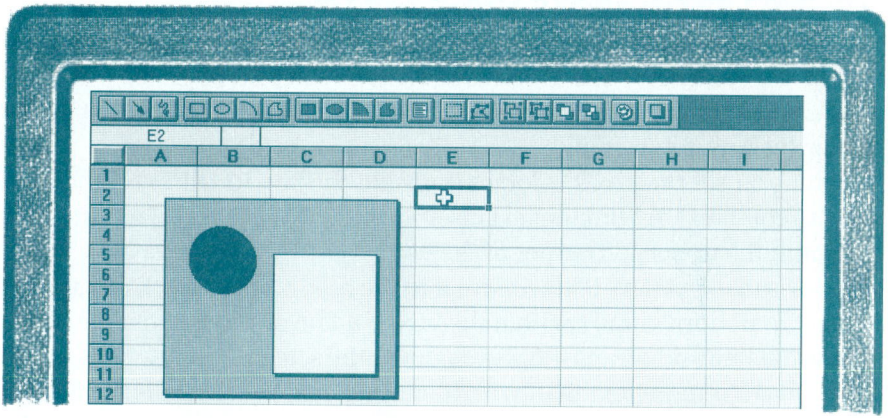

Cell E2 selected as "target" for Paste operation

Choose Paste on the Edit menu. Excel pastes the contents of the Clipboard into the target cell to the right of the original objects. You now see two identical versions of the rectangle, circle, and text box.

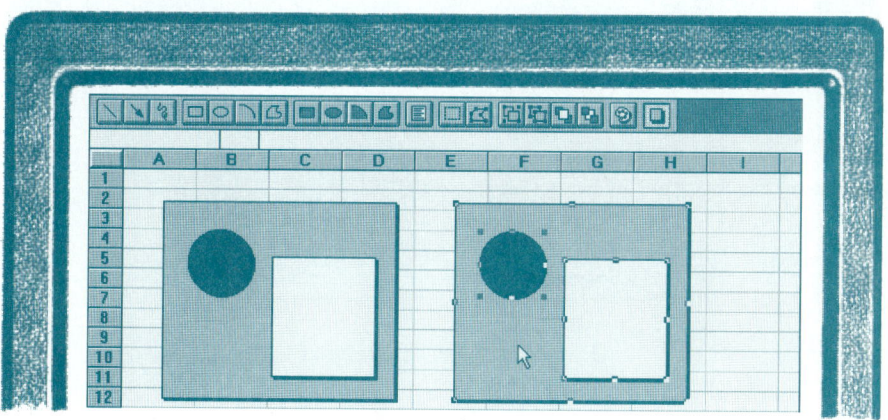

Copy of objects pasted onto the worksheet

Editing Excel Graphic Objects

Select the text box on the right side of the screen. To do so, you may have to first click an empty cell to release currently selected objects.

Select just the text box; then choose the Color tool and set the text box to a color (yellow, for example).

After you set the box's color, click inside the box to tell Excel that you want to enter text. A blinking text insertion cursor (a vertical black line) will appear in the upper-left corner of the box.

Enter some text (any text will do) into the box. Notice how Excel adjusts the text to fit horizontally within the box. If a line of text is too wide, Excel breaks the line and wraps the words down the screen.

If you enter more text than will fit into the box, Excel scrolls the text up the screen. You can click and drag on the contents of the box to view all the entered text.

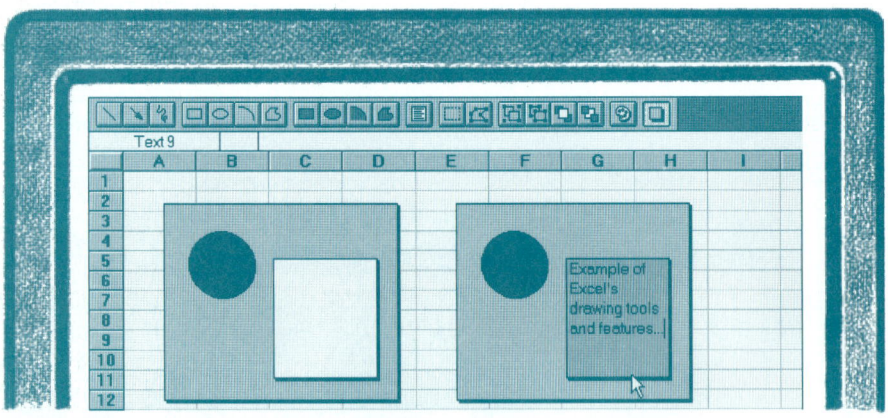

Text and color added to text box

The Excel Slide Show

Excel lets you copy and paste parts of a worksheet onto a slide show document. You can then display those items, one after the other, on the full screen. The result looks like a professional slide show presentation. Any object on an Excel worksheet—including cells, charts, and graphics—can be viewed and displayed in an Excel slide show.

To see how the slide show feature works, select the range of cells that includes the three graphic objects on the left side of the worksheet. To make this selection, click cell A2. Then click and drag from cell A2 to cell D13.

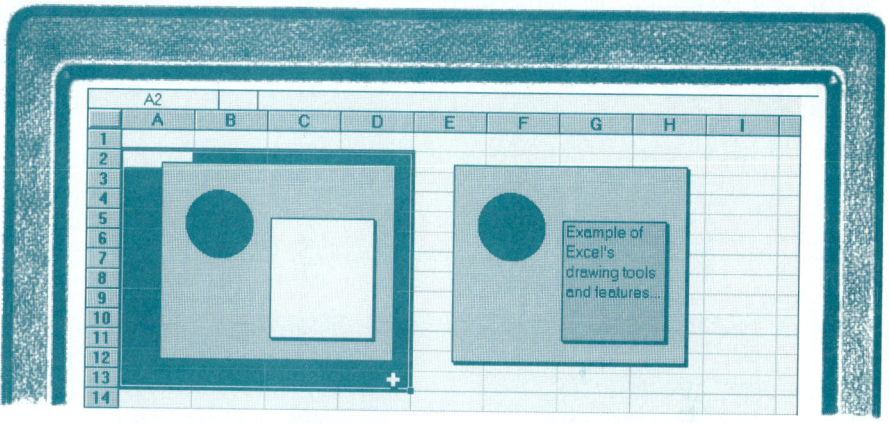

Cells and objects being copied

After you select the indicated cells, pull down the Edit menu and choose Copy to place a copy of the images on the Clipboard. Then choose New on the File menu. You'll see a New dialog box that shows the five available types of Excel documents: worksheets, charts, macro sheets, workbooks, and slides.

Select Slides and click OK.

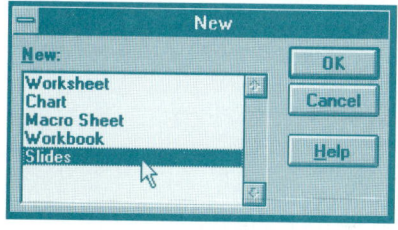

New dialog box

The Slides Worksheet

A new slides worksheet appears.

The worksheet's first two rows show nine buttons. These buttons let you control the editing of slides and the running of a slide show.

Row 3 displays a set of labels that identify the slide image, and the four slide attributes Effect Type, Effect Speed, Slide Advance, and Sound File. You will learn more about these attributes in just a moment.

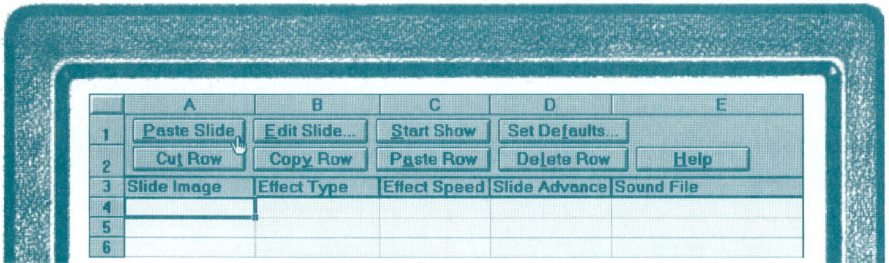

Slide show worksheet before Paste Slide activity

Click the Paste Slide button on the first row of the slide worksheet (cell A1).

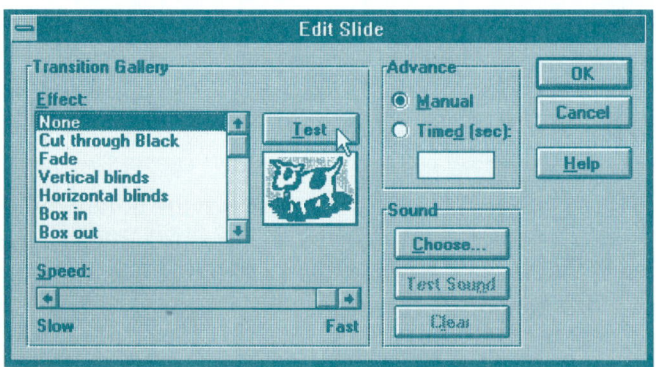

Edit slide dialog box

Excel pastes the contents of the Clipboard onto the worksheet, and brings up the Edit Slide dialog box.

The Edit Slide Dialog Box

On the left side of the dialog box is a list of video effects that can be applied when a slide is brought to the screen. You can preview what an effect looks like by choosing an item from the list and clicking the Test button.

Below the list of effects is the Speed control. This control regulates how fast an effect happens during transitions between two slides. Fast has a value of 10; Slow has a value of 1. A numerical value appears once you select any effect other than None.

The Advance controls to the right of the Test button let you set the Advance mode for the show (Manual or Timed). In Manual mode, you have to click the mouse to move from slide to slide. The Sound controls let you choose a Sound file to be played while the slide is showing.

Note: To use sound in a slide show on an IBM-compatible computer, you must be using Microsoft Windows version 3.1 or later, or else Microsoft Windows version 3.0 with Multimedia Extensions version 1.0 or later. You must also have a sound card installed in your computer. On the Macintosh, you must be using system software 6.0.7 or later.

Move the highlight down the list to the Dissolve Small Blocks effect. Click Test and watch the effect take place. The dog image dissolves into the key image.

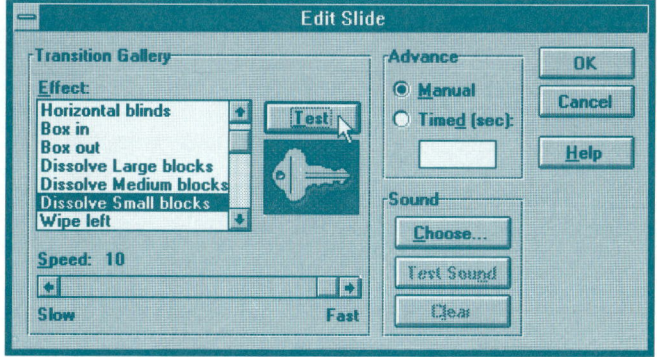

Effect selected and tested

Click OK to accept the video effects, speed, advance mode, and sound settings. Excel dismisses the Edit Slide dialog box. You see the slides worksheet with the first slide stored on row 4.

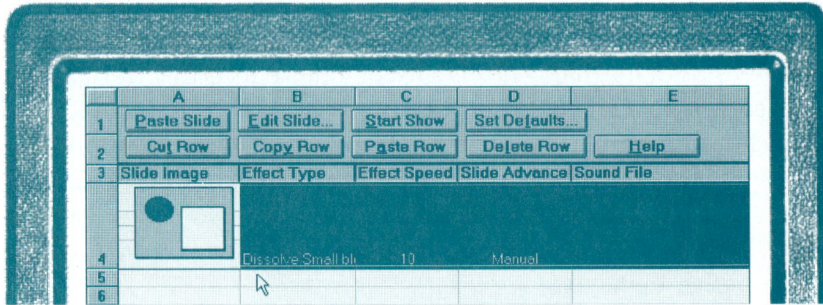

Slide paste operation completed

A reduced image of the slide appears in cell A4. The slide attributes are shown in cells B4, C4, and D4. E4 is blank since there is no attached sound file for this slide.

Add a Second Slide

Use the Window menu and go back to the worksheet that contains the graphic objects. This time, select the cells (E2 through H13) that surround and lie beneath the three graphic objects on the right side of the worksheet.

When the cells are selected, choose Copy on the Edit menu to copy the selection to the Clipboard.

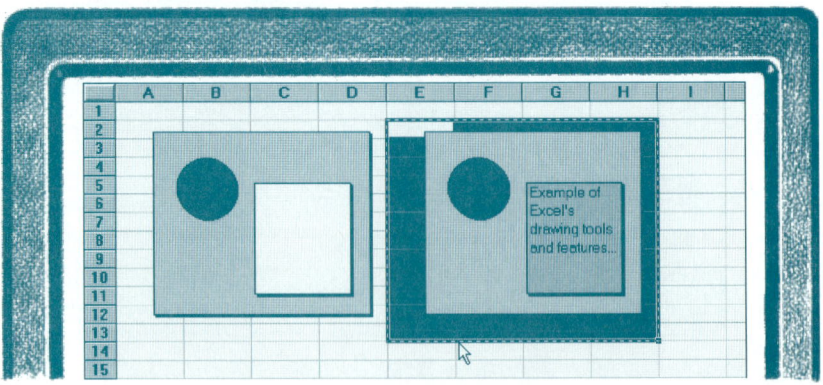

Second set of cells and objects being copied

Use the Window menu and return to the slides worksheet. Click the Paste Slide button to paste the contents of the Clipboard into this worksheet.

You will see the Edit Slide dialog box again. Choose the Dissolve Small Blocks effect for this slide, and click OK to dismiss the dialog box.

A reduced image of the second slide appears in cell A5. That slide's attributes are shown in cells B5 through E5.

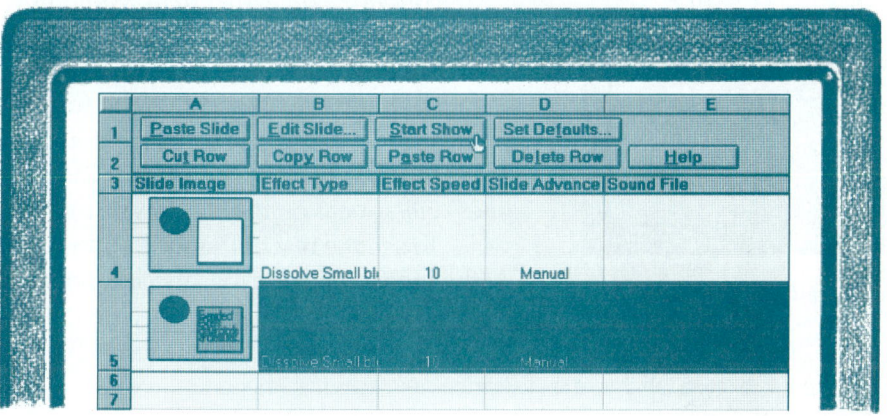

Slide worksheet after second slide has been pasted

Start the Show

Click the Start Show button (cell C1). The Start Show dialog box appears. Click the check box in the upper-left corner to tell Excel that you want to run the slide show until the ESC key is pressed.

Click here to select this option

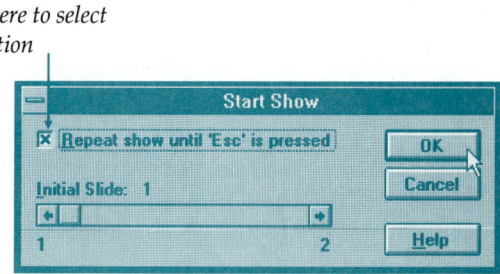

Start Show dialog box

The control on the lower-left corner of the dialog box lets you specify the initial slide. For now, leave it at slide 1, and click OK.

The screen flashes and flickers. The cells and graphic objects that represent the first slide emerge through the dissolve effect. The first segment of the original worksheet that you copied to the Clipboard expands to fill the screen. If the cells on the original worksheet had contained data, that data would now show on the slide. The grid lines for the cells are displayed because they appeared on the original worksheet. If you turn off the grid lines on a worksheet before you copy and paste cells to a slide, no grid lines will appear on the slide show images.

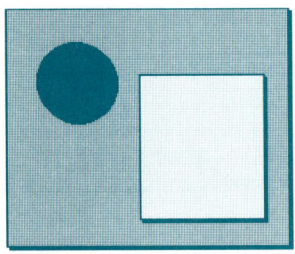

First slide in slide show

To see the rest of the slide show, click the mouse. Excel brings the second slide to the screen using the specified video effect, Dissolve Small Blocks.

Since the two slides are identical except for the text box color and contents, the dissolve appears to happen only within the text box.

When the dissolve completes, you see the complete second slide.

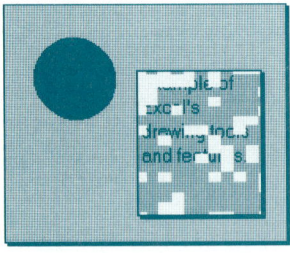 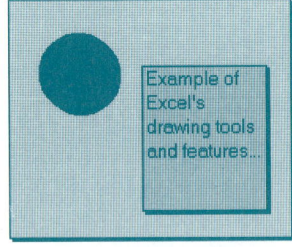

Second slide during and after effect is completed

The slide show continues as long as you keep clicking the mouse. The screen dissolves back to the first slide, presents the second slide again, and so forth. To terminate the slide show, press the ESC key. A Slide Show Options dialog box appears. Click the Stop button to close this dialog box and return to the slides worksheet.

This concludes your tour of Excel's charting and drawing tools. These tools work together to let you:

- Transform data into professional-looking graphic images
- Organize the data and images into impressive slide shows
- Add your own graphic touches and enhancements

Workbooks and Links

7

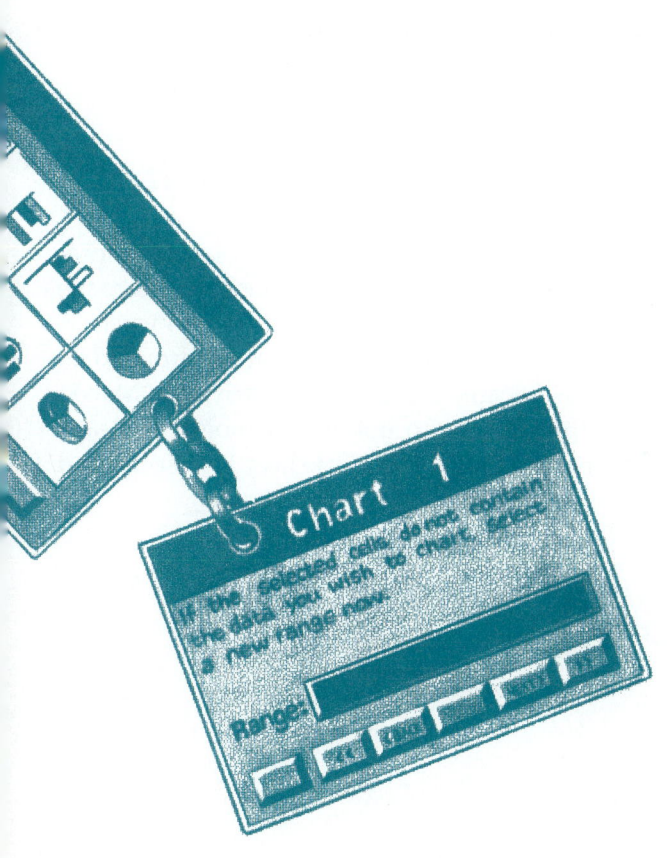

In Chapter 6, "Chart Power," you discovered that information on a worksheet and the chart created from the worksheet data were linked together. If you adjusted the information on the chart, Excel automatically adjusted the corresponding worksheet data. If you adjusted the data, Excel changed the chart.

In this chapter, you will explore Excel's workbook feature, which lets you organize and manage linked collections of Excel worksheets. You will also look more closely at Excel linkages and will discover how you tell Excel to link information between documents explicitly.

The Mileage Worksheet and Chart

One of the authors of this book recently bought an old 1974 Mazda RX4. The car has only been driven 90,000 miles. The author plans to restore the vehicle, and only uses the car occasionally. He usually rides his bicycle.

Last month, it rained almost every day, the temperature dropped to freezing at night, and the roads became icy. He had to drive the Mazda more than normal, but it gave him a chance to look at a full month's mileage data for the car. Of course, he used an Excel worksheet to display and evaluate the data.

	A	B	C	D	E	F	G
1			1974 RX4 Mileage Data				
2	Date	Route	Gallons	Cost	Mileage	CPG	MPG
3	3-Sep	city	5	$6.30	65	1.26	13.00
4	5-Sep	freeway	9	$11.70	160	1.30	17.78
5	7-Sep	combo	11	$14.29	170	1.30	15.45
6	10-Sep	combo	8	$10.45	110	1.31	13.75
7	12-Sep	freeway	10	$12.69	165	1.27	16.50
8	15-Sep	city	5	$6.40	70	1.28	14.00
9	17-Sep	city	6	$7.80	55	1.30	9.17
10	20-Sep	freeway	8	$10.75	130	1.34	16.25
11	24-Sep	combo	9	$11.80	140	1.31	15.56
12	29-Sep	city	7	$8.80	95	1.26	13.57
13	Totals		78	100.98	1160	1.29	14.87

Mileage data worksheet

The worksheet displays the date of each gas purchase (column A). Dates are shown in a day-month (*dd-mmm*) format. You use the Format menu's Number command to access date format options.

The primary type of driving is indicated by the Route information (city, freeway, combo). The number of gallons purchased, the cost for gas, and the number of miles driven since the last gas stop are also recorded (columns C, D, and E). Data in column D are formatted using a currency format option (use the Number command on the Format menu).

The data in columns F and G show the cost per gallon (CPG) and the miles per gallon (MPG), respectively. Data in columns F and G are formatted to show only two decimal places (use the Number command on the Format menu). The results for CPG are computed with formulas that reference the values in columns C and D. For example, the formula =D3/C3 produces the result in cell F3; the formula =D13/C13 produces the result in cell F13.

The MPG results are based on formulas that reference the values in columns C and E. For example, the result in cell G3 is based on the formula =E3/C3; the result in cell G13 is based on the formula =E13/C13.

The results in cells C13, D13, and E13 of the Totals row are sums of the numeric values in each of those columns, respectively. These sums are computed with formulas that use one of Excel's functions called SUM.

Excel Functions

Excel functions are prewritten calculation tools. You can use these tools to simplify your formula-building tasks, and to perform a variety of sophisticated number-crunching jobs.

The formulas in cells C13, D13, and E13 on the mileage data worksheet have been cleared so you can rebuild them, and see how the Excel SUM function works.

Simply Excel

	A	B	C	D	E	F	G
1			1974 RX4 Mileage Data				
2	Date	Route	Gallons	Cost	Mileage	CPG	MPG
3	3-Sep	city	5	$6.30	65	1.26	13.00
4	5-Sep	freeway	9	$11.70	160	1.30	17.78
5	7-Sep	combo	11	$14.29	170	1.30	15.45
6	10-Sep	combo	8	$10.45	110	1.31	13.75
7	12-Sep	freeway	10	$12.69	165	1.27	16.50
8	15-Sep	city	5	$6.40	70	1.28	14.00
9	17-Sep	city	6	$7.80	55	1.30	9.17
10	20-Sep	freeway	8	$10.75	130	1.34	16.25
11	24-Sep	combo	9	$11.80	140	1.31	15.56
12	29-Sep	city	7	$8.80	95	1.26	13.57
13	Totals					#DIV/0!	#DIV/0!
14							

— Division by zero error message

Formulas cleared from cells C13, D13, and E13

Cells F13 and G13 have formulas that use the result in cell C13 as a divisor. Removing the formula in cell C13 causes the contents of C13 to be empty. The empty cell C13 then causes the formulas in cells F13 and G13 to produce "division by zero" error messages (#DIV/0!). When referenced as a numeric constant in a formula, an empty cell is equivalent to a value of zero.

Sum tool

C3   =SUM(C3:C12)

	A	B	C	D	E	F	G
1			1974 RX4 Mileage Data				
2	Date	Route	Gallons	Cost	Mileage	CPG	MPG
3	3-Sep	city	5	$6.30	65	1.26	13.00
4	5-Sep	freeway	9	$11.70	160	1.30	17.78
5	7-Sep	combo	11	$14.29	170	1.30	15.45
6	10-Sep	combo	8	$10.45	110	1.31	13.75
7	12-Sep	freeway	10	$12.69	165	1.27	16.50
8	15-Sep	city	5	$6.40	70	1.28	14.00
9	17-Sep	city	6	$7.80	55	1.30	9.17
10	20-Sep	freeway	8	$10.75	130	1.34	16.25
11	24-Sep	combo	9	$11.80	140	1.31	15.56
12	29-Sep	city	7	$8.80	95	1.26	13.57
13	Totals		M(C3:C12)			#DIV/0!	#DIV/0!
14							
15							

Formula with SUM function in cell C13

To establish the formula for cell C13, click C13, and then click the Sum tool on the standard toolbar.

Excel automatically makes an intelligent guess regarding the range of data you plan to sum (all the numeric data in the column above the selected cell). The program outlines the supposed data range (C3 through C12 or C3:C12 in Excel's shorthand cell range notation) with a set of moving dashes that looks like a parade of marching ants. Excel then attaches the following formula to cell C13:

=SUM(C3:C12)

The equal sign (=) indicates that the entry is a formula. Immediately after the equal sign, you see the name of the function, SUM. After the function's name, a pair of parentheses encloses the function's argument list. *Arguments* are numbers, text, logical values, arrays, or cell references that the function uses to calculate values or perform actions. In this case, the function's arguments are the cell references for the range of data (C3:C12) to be summed.

Note: *Because of the cell width of C13, you only see "M(C3:C12)." To see the whole formula, =SUM(C3:C12), refer to the formula bar.*

The formula with the SUM function represents a concise way of writing this much longer, but equivalent, formula:

=C3+C4+C5+C6+C7+C8+C9+C10+C11+C12

If you click the enter box (the check mark icon) on the formula bar, Excel accepts the proposed formula, and calculates the sum for the outlined data range.

Cells F13 and G13 no longer show a division by zero error message (DIV/0). The value in C13 now causes the formulas in cells F13 and G13 to produce zero values.

	A	B	C	D	E	F	G
1			1974 RX4 Mileage Data				
2	Date	Route	Gallons	Cost	Mileage	CPG	MPG
3	3-Sep	city	5	$6.30	65	1.26	13.00
4	5-Sep	freeway	9	$11.70	160	1.30	17.78
5	7-Sep	combo	11	$14.29	170	1.30	15.45
6	10-Sep	combo	8	$10.45	110	1.31	13.75
7	12-Sep	freeway	10	$12.69	165	1.27	16.50
8	15-Sep	city	5	$6.40	70	1.28	14.00
9	17-Sep	city	6	$7.80	55	1.30	9.17
10	20-Sep	freeway	8	$10.75	130	1.34	16.25
11	24-Sep	combo	9	$11.80	140	1.31	15.56
12	29-Sep	city	7	$8.80	95	1.26	13.57
13	Totals		78			0.00	0.00

Sum calculated for cells C3:C12

The formula attached to cell C13 appears in the formula bar. The calculated result of the formula, 78, appears in cell C13.

Formulas in D13 and E13 take the same form as the one in C13. To attach SUM formulas to cells D13 and E13, use the fill handle on the lower-right corner of cell C13. Click and drag the fill handle of cell C13 to the right. Drag the outline across to cell E13 and then release the mouse button. Values will appear in cells D13 and E13. Cells F13 and G13 now show values based on the results in cells C13, D13, and E13.

	A	B	C	D	E	F	G
1			1974 RX4 Mileage Data				
2	Date	Route	Gallons	Cost	Mileage	CPG	MPG
3	3-Sep	city	5	$6.30	65	1.26	13.00
4	5-Sep	freeway	9	$11.70	160	1.30	17.78
5	7-Sep	combo	11	$14.29	170	1.30	15.45
6	10-Sep	combo	8	$10.45	110	1.31	13.75
7	12-Sep	freeway	10	$12.69	165	1.27	16.50
8	15-Sep	city	5	$6.40	70	1.28	14.00
9	17-Sep	city	6	$7.80	55	1.30	9.17
10	20-Sep	freeway	8	$10.75	130	1.34	16.25
11	24-Sep	combo	9	$11.80	140	1.31	15.56
12	29-Sep	city	7	$8.80	95	1.26	13.57
13	Totals		78	100.98	1160	1.29	14.87

Fill handle used to copy formulas

The fill handle copied the formula in cell C13 to the two adjacent cells. During the copy operation, the cell references in the formula were adjusted to correspond to the two new locations. The result is a set of three formulas that calculate totals based on the data in the columns above the formulas.

Cell	Formula
C13	=SUM(C3:C12)
D13	=SUM(D3:D12)
E13	=SUM(E3:E12)

Chart the Mileage Data

To set up the worksheets for the rest of this chapter, some of the mileage data will be charted and saved as a separate document. To begin the charting operation, select the indicated data in the MPG column (G2:G12). Include the label in cell G2, and exclude the summary value in cell G13.

	A	B	C	D	E	F	G	H	I
1			1974 RX4 Mileage Data						
2	Date	Route	Gallons	Cost	Mileage	CPG	MPG		
3	3-Sep	city	5	$6.30	65	1.26	13.00		
4	5-Sep	freeway	9	$11.70	160	1.30	17.78		
5	7-Sep	combo	11	$14.29	170	1.30	15.45		
6	10-Sep	combo	8	$10.45	110	1.31	13.75		
7	12-Sep	freeway	10	$12.69	165	1.27	16.50		
8	15-Sep	city	5	$6.40	70	1.28	14.00		
9	17-Sep	city	6	$7.80	55	1.30	9.17		
10	20-Sep	freeway	8	$10.75	130	1.34	16.25		
11	24-Sep	combo	9	$11.80	140	1.31	15.56		
12	29-Sep	city	7	$8.80	95	1.26	13.57		
13	Totals		78	100.98	1160	1.29	14.87		
14									

MPG data to be charted

Now, select the data in the Date column as well. Include the label in cell A2; exclude the label in cell A13. To form this nonadjacent selection, hold down the CTRL key (use the Command key on the Macintosh), and click and drag the mouse pointer from cell A2 to cell A12.

	A	B	C	D	E	F	G	H	I
1			1974 RX4 Mileage Data						
2	Date	Route	Gallons	Cost	Mileage	CPG	MPG		
3	3-Sep	city	5	$6.30	65	1.26	13.00		
4	5-Sep	freeway	9	$11.70	160	1.30	17.78		
5	7-Sep	combo	11	$14.29	170	1.30	15.45		
6	10-Sep	combo	8	$10.45	110	1.31	13.75		
7	12-Sep	freeway	10	$12.69	165	1.27	16.50		
8	15-Sep	city	5	$6.40	70	1.28	14.00		
9	17-Sep	city	6	$7.80	55	1.30	9.17		
10	20-Sep	freeway	8	$10.75	130	1.34	16.25		
11	24-Sep	combo	9	$11.80	140	1.31	15.56		
12	29-Sep	city	7	$8.80	95	1.26	13.57		
13	Totals		78	100.98	1160	1.29	14.87		
14									

Column A data to be used for chart axis

The Date information (column A) will be used to mark an axis on the chart. Click the ChartWizard tool on the standard toolbar (the second icon from the right end of the toolbar).

Two parades of marching ants surround the selected cells in columns A and G. ChartWizard waits for you to identify the region on the worksheet where you want to place the chart.

Click and drag with the mouse to create a chart region. You can put this region anywhere on the chart. In the example, the chart region overlaps the worksheet cells.

Chapter 7: Workbooks and Links   **137**

	A	B	C	D	E	F	G	H	I
1			1974 RX4 Mileage Data						
2	Date	Route	Gallons	Cost	Mileage	CPG	MPG		
3	3-Sep	city	5	$6.30	65	1.26	13.00		
4	5-Sep	freeway	9	$11.70	160	1.30	17.78		
5	7-Sep	combo	11	$14.29	170	1.30	15.45		
6	10-Sep	combo	8	$10.45	110	1.31	13.75		
7	12-Sep	freeway	10	$12.69	165	1.27	16.50		
8	15-Sep	city	5	$6.40	70	1.28	14.00		
9	17-Sep	city	6	$7.80	55	1.30	9.17		
10	20-Sep	freeway	8	$10.75	130	1.34	16.25		
11	24-Sep	combo	9	$11.80	140	1.31	15.56		
12	29-Sep	city	7	$8.80	95	1.26	13.57		
13	Totals		78	100.98	1160	1.29	14.87		

ChartWizard activated and chart region being selected

When you release the mouse button, the first ChartWizard dialog box appears. This dialog box asks you to confirm the data range being used in the chart. A glance at the Range text box shows absolute references to the following cells: A2 through A12 ($A$2:$A$12) and G2 through G12 ($G$2:$G$12)—the cells you selected on the worksheet.

Click the Next button to accept the data range. A second ChartWizard dialog box appears that lets you select the type of chart to be used.

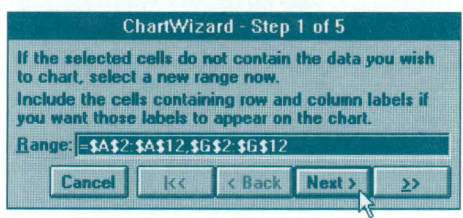

First ChartWizard dialog box

138 Simply Excel

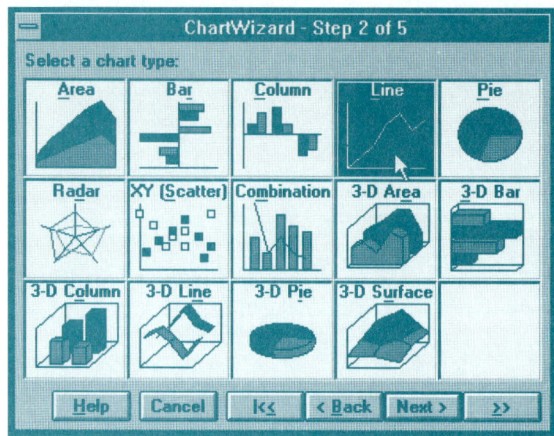

Selection of Line chart

When the dialog box appears, ChartWizard picks the column chart as the default selection. For this example, you will use the line chart. Click the Line chart image, and then click Next to confirm this setting and display the third ChartWizard dialog box.

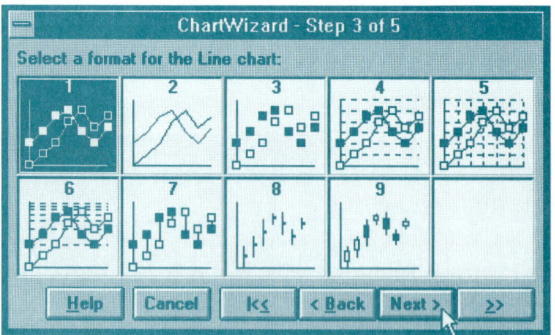

Line chart format selected

This ChartWizard dialog box lets you choose a format for the line chart. Click Next to accept the ChartWizard's default format setting—a line chart with the data points marked with a symbol. The fourth dialog box appears.

In this dialog box, you help ChartWizard interpret the data. ChartWizard assumes the data are in columns (correct), and that the first column of data is to be used for X-axis labels (also correct).

ChartWizard initially assumes that the first row of data contains the First Data Point (incorrect). Click the Legend Text option under Use First Row For to tell ChartWizard how to use the first row of data. ChartWizard adjusts the Sample Chart immediately to reflect this new setting.

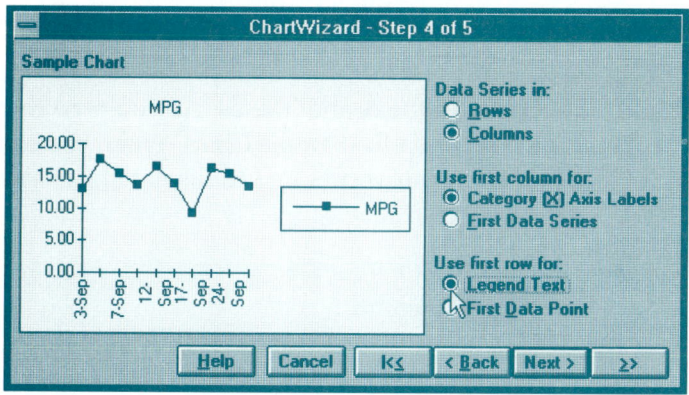

ChartWizard told how to interpret data

After you tell ChartWizard how to interpret the data, click Next to see the final ChartWizard dialog box.

You use this dialog box to add and remove the legend box, and to enter titles for the chart and the chart's axes. Click the No option to remove the legend box. Since there is only one category of data being charted, no legend is required.

Legend and title selections made

Enter titles for the chart and the X and Y axes. As you type each title, ChartWizard displays the entry on the Sample Chart. When you complete the titles, click OK to confirm your entries and to display the chart on the worksheet.

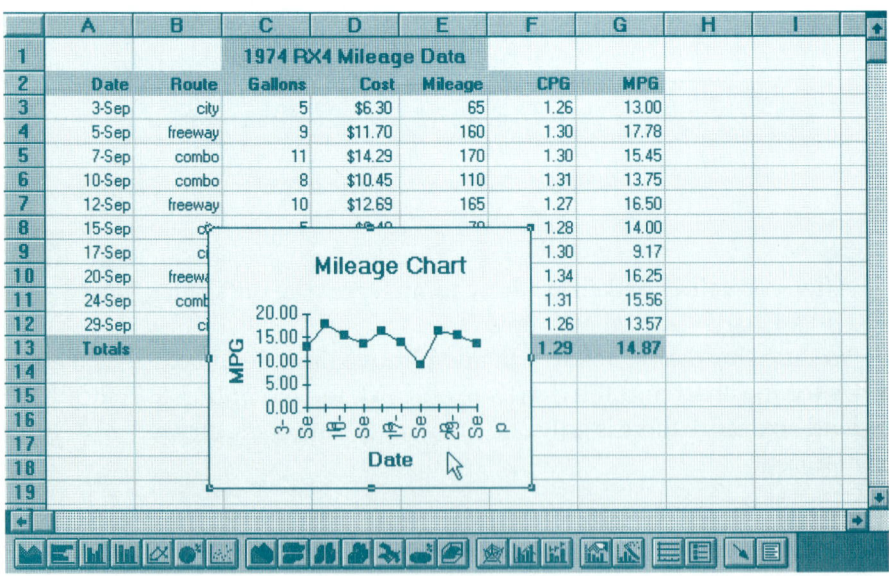

Worksheet with embedded chart

A chart created in this way is said to be embedded in the worksheet. An object that is *embedded* in a worksheet is part of that document. It can be moved, sized, and edited like any other part of the worksheet.

For example, the X-axis labels on the embedded chart are "scrunched" together on the display. If you wish, use the black selection handles on the border of the chart to expand the chart region, and make the X-axis labels easier to read.

Save the Worksheet and the Chart

You can also save an embedded chart as a separate Excel document. To do so, let's first save the worksheet including its embedded chart, in case we make a mistake and have to start over. Choose the Save As command on the File menu.

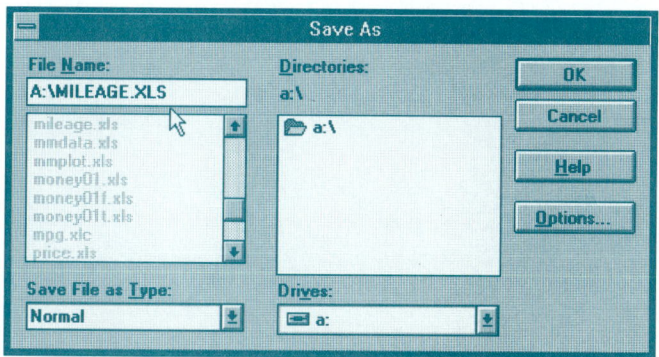

Save As dialog box while saving worksheet

The Save As dialog box lets you save the current worksheet under a filename of your choice. For this example, suppose you want to:

- Name the file MILEAGE
- Record the fact that the file is an Excel worksheet
- Save the worksheet on a formatted, floppy disk that you have placed into drive A on your computer

You can perform these tasks directly by typing

A:\MILEAGE.XLS

into the File Name text box and clicking the OK button.

The first three characters of the text box entry (A:\) tell Excel that you want to save the file on drive A. You indicate that the file name is MILEAGE. The file extension (.XLS) identifies the file as a worksheet.

Excel uses five file extension codes to organize and identify different types of Excel files:

Extension	Type of File
.XLS	Worksheet
.XLC	Chart
.XLW	Workbook
.XLM	Macro
.XLT	Template

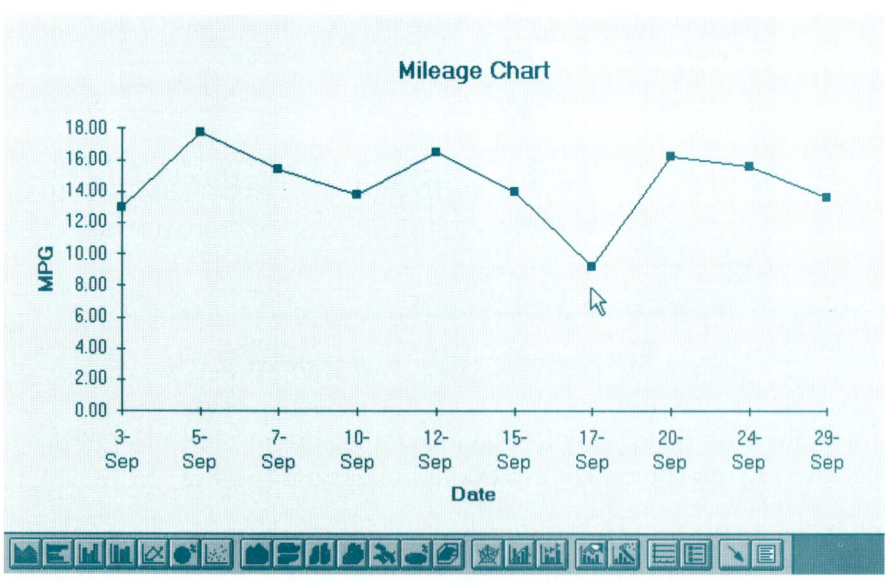

Chart in its own window

In just a few moments, you will use and save chart and workbook files with .XLC and .XLW extensions. For more information about Excel files, refer to Appendix C, "The Excel 4.0 Environment."

After you save the worksheet, double-click the embedded chart to put the chart in its own window.

Make sure that there is a formatted, floppy disk in drive A. Then choose the Save As command on the File menu. When the Save As dialog box appears, type the following entry into the File Name text box:

A:\MPG.XLC

This entry will save the chart onto the floppy disk in drive A. The file name will be MPG. The file extension, .XLC, identifies the file as an Excel chart. Click OK to save the chart.

After you save the chart in its own file, use the Window menu to return to the worksheet window (MILEAGE.XLS). The embedded chart may still be selected. If it is not, click the chart to select it. Then press DEL to remove the chart from this worksheet.

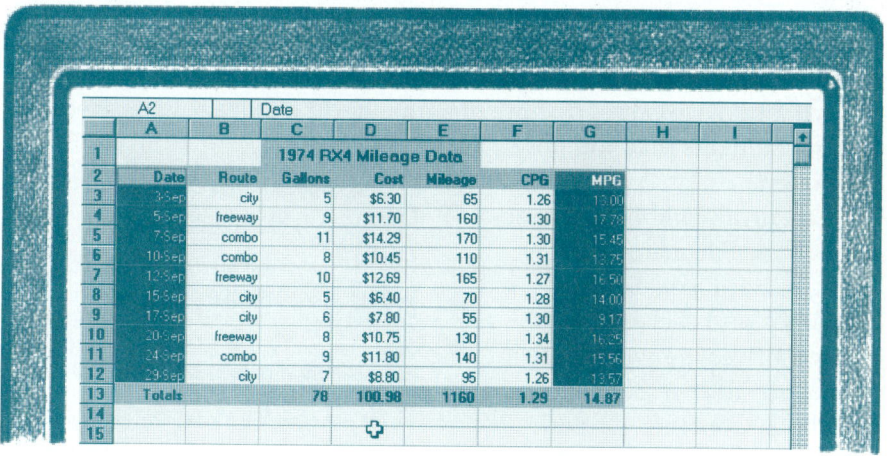

Worksheet with chart deleted

If you now check the Window menu, you will see that the mileage worksheet is the only active Excel document. Removing the embedded chart forced Excel to close the chart window. The chart is not lost; you saved it in the file MPG.XLC.

Use the Save command on the File menu, and save this version of the mileage worksheet that does not have a chart.

Load the Chart from the Disk

Use the Open command on the File menu, and open the chart file MPG.XLC. The Open command displays an Open dialog box that you can use to locate and open the required file. Open MPG.XLC.

You now have two separate Excel documents open and ready for use: MPG.XLC and MILEAGE.XLS. MPG.XLC is the active document.

Excel Workbook Features

Excel has a special type of document, called a workbook, that helps you organize and use other Excel documents. To experiment with this feature, you will build a *workbook* document to manage the mileage worksheet and chart documents that you now have open.

To create a workbook, choose New on the File menu. A New dialog box appears. Select Workbook and click OK.

Excel displays a workbook document. You see the Workbook Contents window.

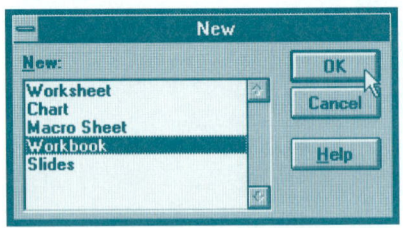

New dialog box with Workbook selected

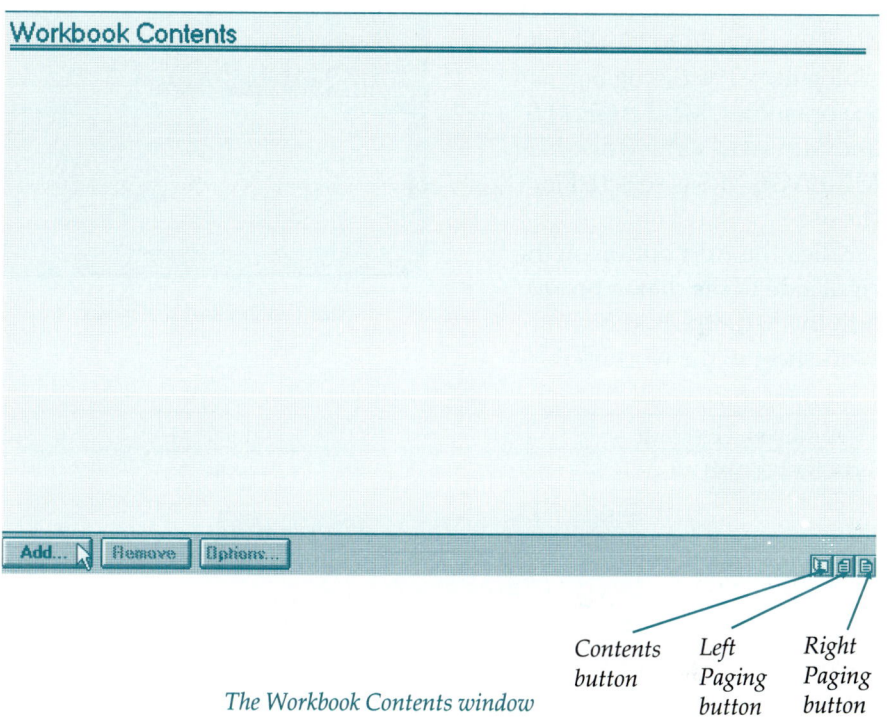

The Workbook Contents window

The Contents window has three buttons in the lower-left corner: Add, Remove, and Options. Since there are no documents in the workbook right now, Add is the only active button. You will soon use this button to add the mileage worksheet and chart documents to the workbook.

In the lower-right corner of the window, you see three small paging buttons. You will use these buttons to page through the documents you put into the workbook. The first button takes you to the Workbook Contents window. The middle button is the Left Paging control for browsing backwards through the list of work-book documents. The right button is the Right Paging control for browsing forward through the document list.

Click the Add button. Excel displays an Add to Workbook dialog box. The dialog box lists the open files, MILEAGE.XLS and MPG.XLC. The worksheet MILEAGE.XLS is selected in the list.

Click the Add button on the right side of the dialog box to add the MILEAGE.XLS worksheet to the workbook.

Add To Workbook dialog box

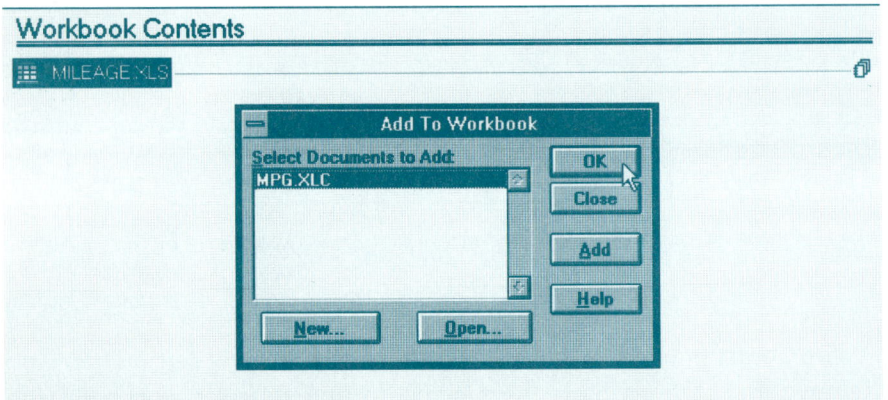

Worksheet added to workbook

When you clicked the Add button on the dialog box, Excel listed the selected file, MILEAGE.XLS, in the Workbook Contents window, and removed that filename from the dialog box.

Now select the chart filename, MPG.XLC, in the dialog box list, and click OK. This action dismisses the dialog box, and lists the chart document as a second workbook entry in the Contents window.

Chapter 7: Workbooks and Links

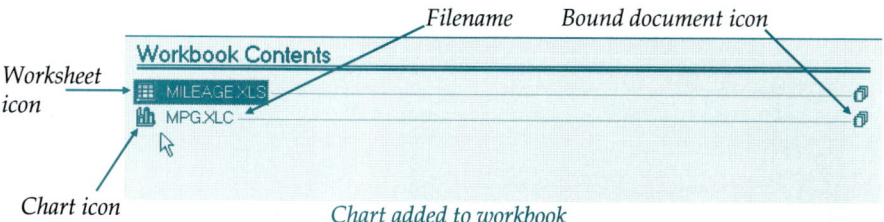

Chart added to workbook

In a Workbook Contents window, each document listing shows three items: an icon for the type of document being listed, a filename, and an icon that indicates whether or not the document is bound into the workbook.

For this example, the listing for MILEAGE.XLS shows a worksheet icon to the left of the worksheet file name. The listing for MPG.XLC shows a chart icon.

The bound document icons on the right side of the screen indicate that both of the documents you added to the workbook are now bound into this workbook. Excel automatically binds a document into a workbook unless you click its bound document icon to unbind it.

Once you save a workbook with bound documents, these bound documents become part of the workbook file, and can only be accessed through the workbook.

Documents that can be accessed by several users, or from several workbooks, can be marked as unbound. An unbound document is not stored as part of the workbook file, but still appears on the Workbook Contents window. To mark a document as unbound, you click that document's icon on the right side of the screen. For the current example, both documents will be bound into the workbook.

Click the Right Paging button to display the first workbook document. The screen shifts instantly to the mileage worksheet window. Since this document is now part of a workbook, the paging controls appear in the lower-right corner of the worksheet window.

148 Simply Excel

	A	B	C	D	E	F	G	H	I
1			1974 RX4 Mileage Data						
2	Date	Route	Gallons	Cost	Mileage	CPG	MPG		
3	3-Sep	city	5	$6.30	65	1.26	13.00		
4	5-Sep	freeway	9	$11.70	160	1.30	17.78		
5	7-Sep	combo	11	$14.29	170	1.30	15.45		
6	10-Sep	combo	8	$10.45	110	1.31	13.75		
7	12-Sep	freeway	10	$12.69	165	1.27	16.50		
8	15-Sep	city	5	$6.40	70	1.28	14.00		
9	17-Sep	city	6	$7.80	55	1.30	9.17		
10	20-Sep	freeway	8	$10.75	130	1.34	16.25		
11	24-Sep	combo	9	$11.80	140	1.31	15.56		
12	29-Sep	city	7	$8.80	95	1.26	13.57		
13	Totals		78	100.98	1160	1.29	14.87		
14									
15									
16									
17									
18									
19									
20									
21									

Right Paging button displayed this worksheet

Click the Right Paging button again. The display now shows the chart window. Here again, the workbook's paging controls are attached to the chart window.

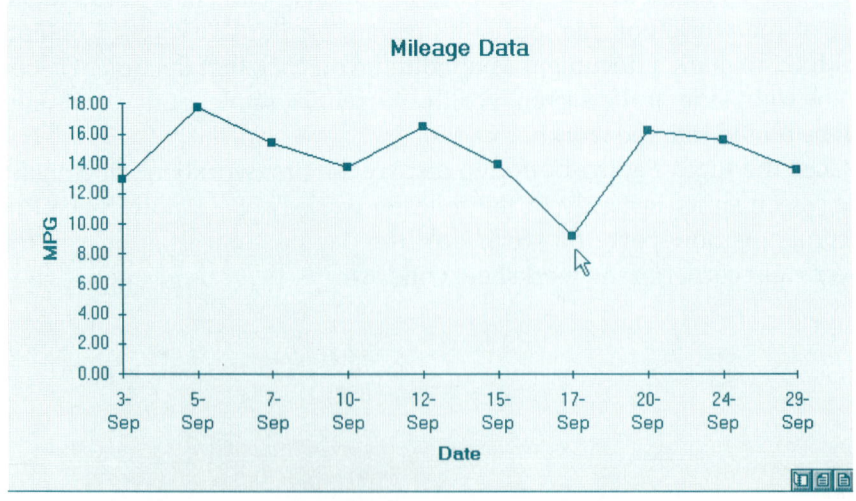

Right paging button displayed the chart

What happens if you now click the Left Paging button? You will see the mileage worksheet once again. What happens if you click the Contents button? The display shows the Workbook Contents window. Try using all three paging buttons on your own. Imagine how handy this workbook feature would be if you had to access and manage a workbook filled with several documents.

Excel Links

In looking over the chart, the author notices that the September 17th entry looks odd. He knows the car does not get great gas mileage, but the MPG for that date looks suspiciously low.

After reviewing the raw data, the author discovers that he made a transcription error when he created the mileage worksheet. Both the date and the number of miles are incorrect.

He uses the paging controls and switches to the mileage worksheet window. He changes the date in cell A9 to the 18th of September, and changes the mileage in cell E9 to 80. This last entry causes the results in G9, and the CPG and MPG Totals, to change.

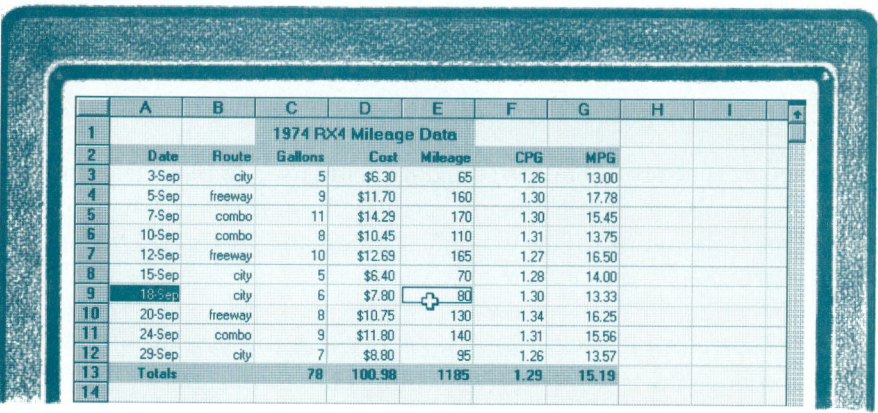

Worksheet data changed

He uses the paging controls (Right Paging button), and switches back to the chart display. Notice that the changes he made to the worksheet appear in the chart. The date on the chart now shows "18-Sep." The MPG value for that date reflects the change to the mileage that he made in the table.

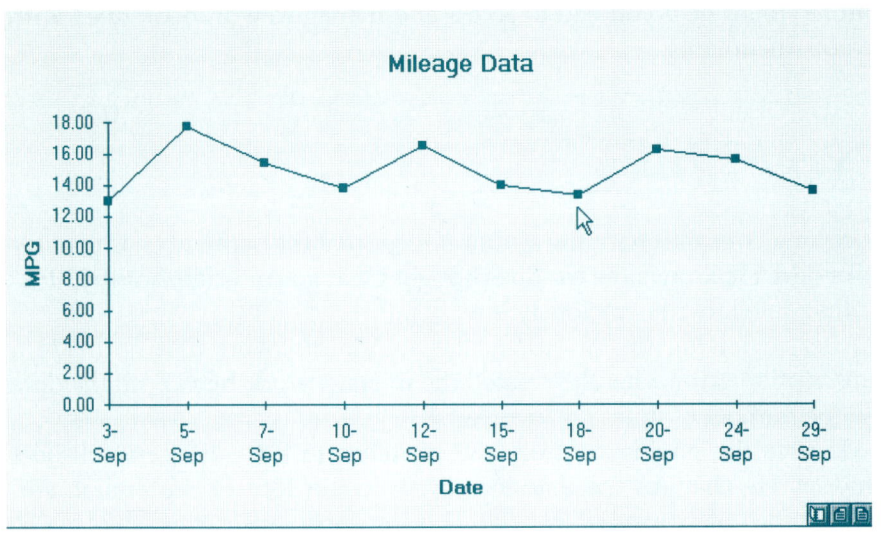

Changes on worksheet reflected on chart

Since the chart was originally created from the worksheet data, the chart contains links to the worksheet. Excel maintained those linkages even though the two documents were put into separate windows, and saved in separate files.

The linkages apply not only to the data being used to plot the points on the chart, but also to the data being used for the axis labels. Changing an entry in the Date column of the worksheet automatically changes that entry on the chart's X axis.

Excel generated all of the embedded links as the chart was being created. You can also control Excel linkages directly. For example, select the chart's title, and change the text entry on the formula bar to an equal sign (=). This action tells Excel that you plan to enter a formula that will compute the title of the chart.

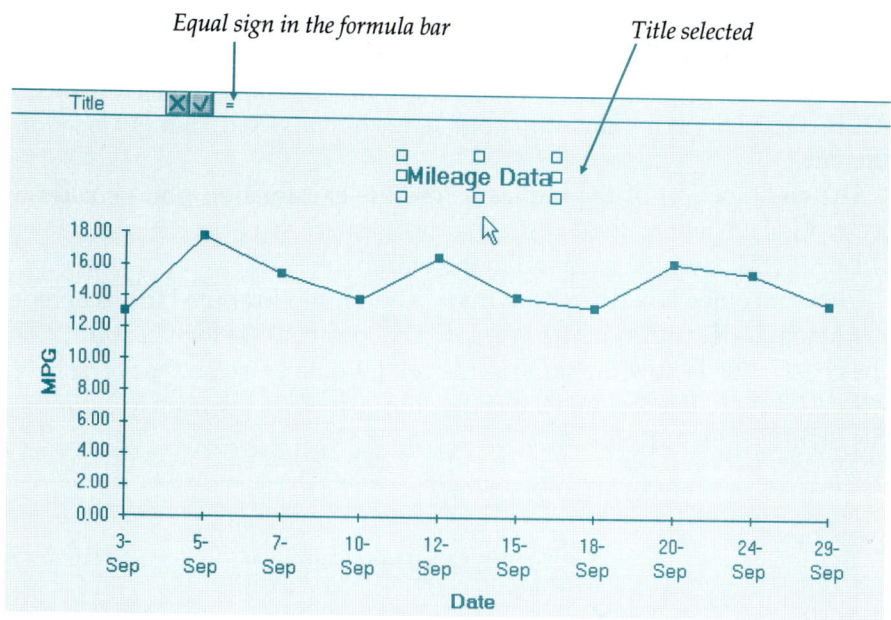

Chart title being linked to worksheet

With the chart title selected and an equal sign on the formula bar, click the Left Paging control. You see the worksheet window. The formula bar still shows the equal sign.

Click the worksheet title (which is centered across cell D1 in the example). The formula bar shows the following formula:

=[Book1]MILEAGE.XLS!$D$1

Data to be linked selected on worksheet

Most of this formula is a reference to the document location for the information in cell D1. The data in brackets, [Book1], is the temporary name of the current workbook document. Next comes the name of the worksheet, MILEAGE.XLS. An exclamation point (!) terminates the document location reference.

The combination of the names before the exclamation point creates a description of where the $D$1 data are located. It is on the worksheet MILEAGE.XLS, which is bound in the workbook Book1.

Click the enter box (the check mark icon on the formula bar) to accept this formula description. The window changes back to the chart display. The chart's title is now the same as the cell D1 data entry on the worksheet MILEAGE.XLS. The formula bar shows the formula being used to compute this title.

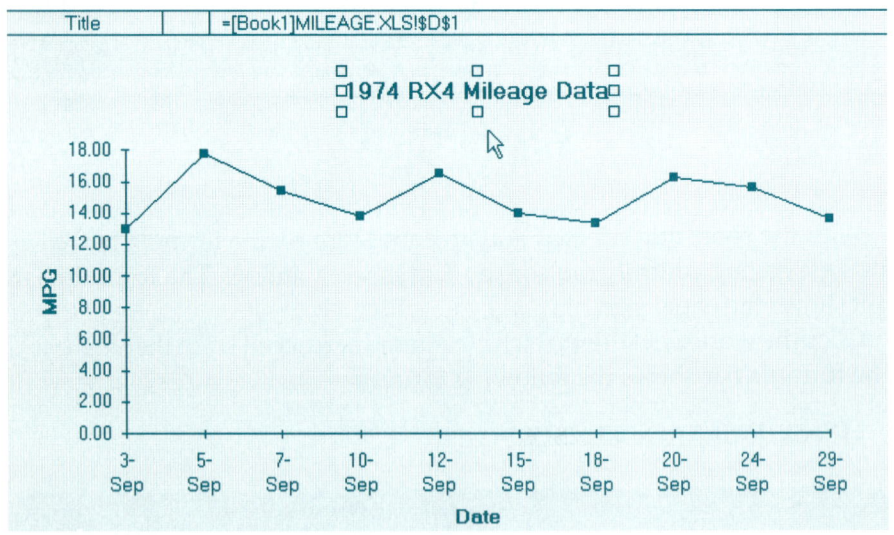

Linked data transferred to chart

You have created a direct link between the title information on the two documents. You created the link by telling Excel where you wanted the linked data, and which data you wanted to link. Excel generated the appropriate formula to make the link work.

Save and Close the Workbook

To save the workbook with its two bound files, choose the Save Workbook command on the File menu. You'll see a Save As dialog box. Make sure there is a formatted, floppy disk in drive A. Then, type

A:\MPGBOOK.XLW

into the File Name text box and click OK.

The workbook document will be saved under the filename MPGBOOK.XLW. The two bound files in the workbook are also saved at the same time, as part of the workbook.

You now have two copies of the mileage worksheet and charted data. Your original versions are stored on disk under the names MILEAGE.XLS and MPG.XLC. The new versions, with the changes you made to the worksheet and the chart, are bound into the workbook, MPGBOOK.XLW.

If you choose the Close Workbook command on the File menu at this time, Excel closes the workbook and its two bound documents. To view the contents of the MPGBOOK.XLW workbook again, you would use the File menu's Open command.

You have completed your initial examination of Excel's workbook and linkage features. Before proceeding to the next topic, you are encouraged to continue your explorations of Excel's unique workbook capabilities on your own. For example, the worksheet and charts of multimedia revenues that you saw in earlier chapters would make an ideal set of linked workbook documents. For practice, you might try your hand at creating an Excel workbook that contains both of those documents.

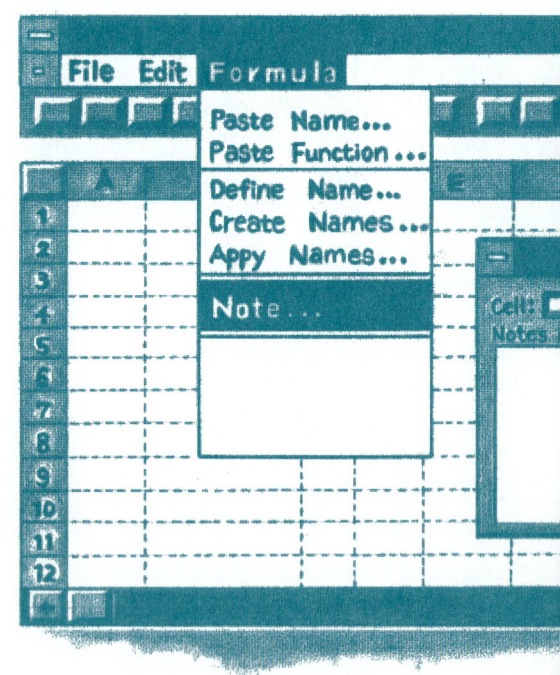

Notes and Other Features

8

Simply Excel

In Chapter 4, "Excel Databases," you watched Katy build a database of Country & Western music. In this chapter, Katy uses that database to examine the Excel Note feature. The Note feature lets her attach text and audio comments to any cell on the worksheet.

After exploring the Excel Note feature with Katy, you will take a more detailed look at Excel toolbars. You will discover how you can use and customize toolbars to match your particular calculation tasks.

Take Note!

Katy uses the margins of her old pencil-and-paper database for notes and comments about the music on each tape. Of course, after a while, these jottings fill the margins and become somewhat jumbled.

Katy looks back at her Country & Western database. She wants to try out the Excel Note feature, and compare it with her pencil-and-paper system.

	A	B	C	D	E	F	G	H
1			Country & Western Tape/Dance Database					
2	Tape #	Artist		Title	Rank	Speed	Dance 1	Dance 2	Dance 3
3	100	Eddie Raven	The Island	5	slow	Cha Cha		
4	101	Dwight Yoakam	Little Ways	3	medium	Two Step	Swing	
5	102	KT Oslin	Cornell Crawford	1	medium	Alley Cat	Horseshoe Special	Schottische
6	103	Hank Williams, Jr.	Born to Boogie	1	fast	Bocephus	Bonanza	Prancing Pony
7	104	Rockin Sydney	Jalapena Lena	1	fast	Flying 8	Two Step	Walkin Wazi
8	105	Kentucky Headhunters	Sixteen and Single	2	medium	Alley Cat	Schottische	Swing
9	106	Waylon Jennings	Lufenbach Texas	2	medium	Cha Cha		
10	107	Travis Tritt	Country Club	2	slow	Two Step	Horseshoe Special	Wooden Nickel
11	108	Garth Brooks	Not Counting You	2	medium	Two Step	Cowboy Boogie	Flying 8
12	109	Bellamy Brothers	Red Neck Girl	4	medium	Tush Push	Sixteen Step	Ten Step
13	110	Steve Warner	Lynda	1	fast	Walkin Wazi	Tush Push	Flying 8
14	111	Jerry Jeff Walker	Trashy Women	1	medium	Tush Push	Two Step	Flying 8
15	112	Hank Williams, Jr.	Old Habits	3	medium	Waltz		
16	113	Kathy Mattea	Going Gone	2	fast	Wooden Nickel	Two Step	Cha Cha
17	114	Mary Chapin Carpenter	Slow Country Dance	1	medium	Waltz		
18								

Country & Western database

After Katy loads the database, she clicks cell A3 to make it the active cell. Cell A3 contains the number of the cassette tape for the first database entry. She plans to attach a note to cell A3 that will be a comment about this tape.

The Excel Text Note Feature

To activate the Excel Note feature, she opens the Formula menu and chooses the Note command.

Excel displays the Cell Note dialog box. Katy will use this dialog box to record a text note about the music. The Cell text box displays the cell (A3) to which the note will be attached. The Notes in Sheet list box is empty because, as yet, the worksheet contains no notes.

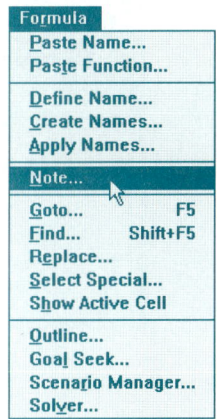

Note command on the Formula menu

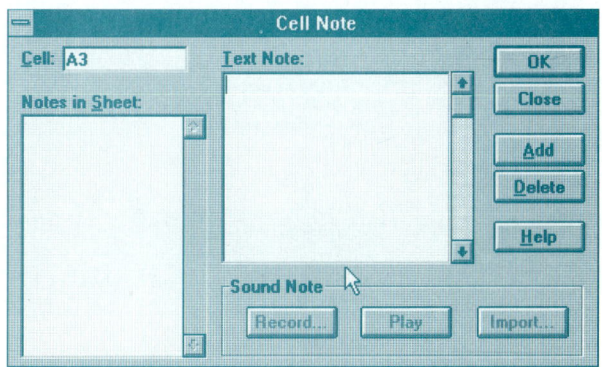

Cell Note dialog box

Katy sees a blinking text insertion point (vertical bar) in the Text Note text box. She enters her note for tape 100 into that text box.

Note that on her PC, Katy creates the blank line between the first line of her note and the third line by pressing CTRL-ENTER at the end of the first and second lines. She does so because if she presses the ENTER key only, she closes the dialog box. On a Macintosh, she would enter line spaces by pressing Option-Return.

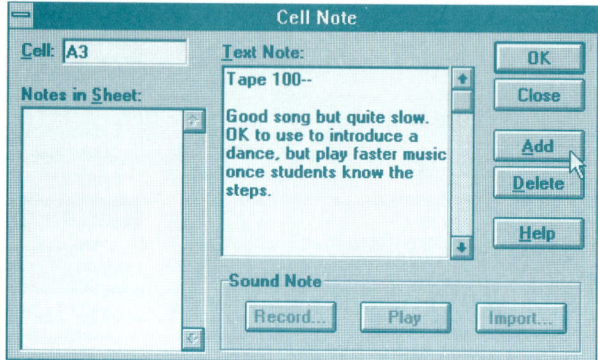

Note for tape 100

To attach the note to the indicated cell (A3), Katy clicks the Add button. The Notes in Sheet list box now shows that cell A3 has an attached note.

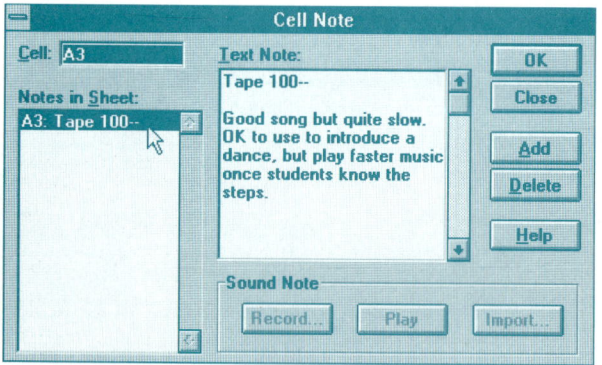

Note added to cell A3

The list entry in the Notes in Sheet list box displays the cell to which the note is attached (A3), a colon (:), and the initial characters from the first line of the note ("Tape 100--").

Katy kept the first line of the note short, and related the text to the cell contents. The body of her note is clear and legible in the Text Note area. If required, her note could be longer and more detailed. Katy already sees several advantages of Excel notes over her messy, and limited, paper-and-pencil system.

Chapter 8: Notes and Other Features 159

She changes the entry in the Cell text box to A4. She then deletes the Tape 100 note in the Text Note text box, and enters a new note for cell A4. The text for this note refers to tape 101.

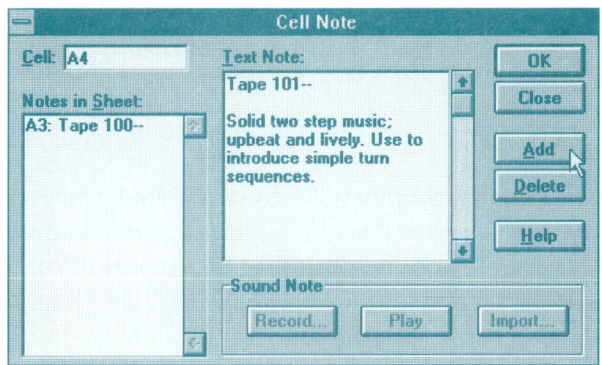

Note for tape 101

After she completes the entry of text for this note, she clicks the Add button to attach the note to cell A4.

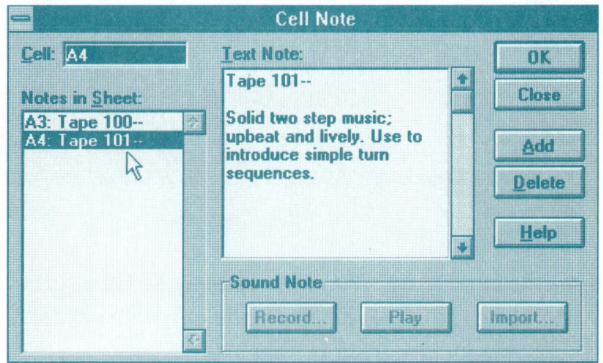

Note added to cell A4

The Notes in Sheet list box now shows two entries, one for cell A3, and a new entry for cell A4. Katy decides to look at the worksheet to see how Excel identifies the cells that have notes attached. She clicks the OK button on the dialog box to return to the worksheet window.

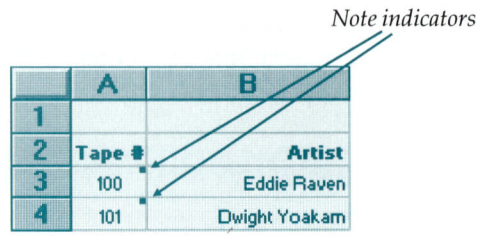

Worksheet cells with note indicators

Excel marks cells that contain notes by displaying a *note indicator symbol* in their upper-right corners. The note indicator symbol appears as a small red box on Katy's screen. Cells A3 and A4 have note indicator symbols.

To see the note attached to cell A3, Katy double-clicks that cell. The Cell Note dialog box appears, with the cell A3 note displayed.

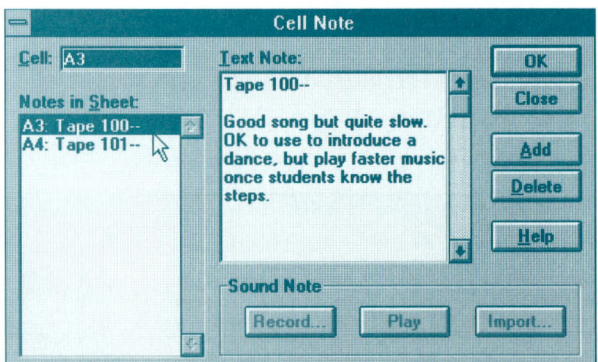

Cell Note dialog box

Katy can read the note for cell A3, and browse through other notes that are listed in the Notes in Sheet list box. She can also edit any existing note, and enter new notes for other worksheet cells.

Play it Again...

Excel also lets you attach sound notes to a worksheet cell. *Sound notes* are recorded audio information. A sound note can be a mixture of spoken words, music, or sound effects. Users can listen to sound notes. In effect, an Excel worksheet cell can "talk" or "sing" to a user.

To use Excel's sound feature on an IBM-compatible computer, you must have a sound board installed in your system. You must also be using Microsoft Windows version 3.0 with Multimedia Extensions version 1.0 or later, or Microsoft Windows version 3.1 or later. On a Macintosh, you must be using system software 6.0.7 or later. For more information on sound notes, refer to the *Microsoft Excel User's Guide 1*.

If your computer can utilize Excel's sound feature, the Sound Note buttons on the Cell Note dialog box will be active. You can then record (and erase) sounds, play sounds that are attached to cells, and import sounds from external audio libraries.

Excel marks a cell with a sound note by inserting an asterisk beside its listing in the Notes in Sheet list box. For example, if cell A3 had a sound note to accompany its current text note, its listing entry would appear as follows:

A3:*Tape 100—

If a cell has a sound note, double-clicking that cell opens the Cell Note dialog box and automatically plays the sound note.

Katy knows exactly what type of sound notes she wants to put in her database. She wants to record each song's introduction, along with her voice-over giving the exact count that starts the dance and the first few words she uses as dance cues. These sound notes will let her quickly review not only the music, but how she starts and cues each dance.

Notes and Other Features

Summary

In this book, you have taken a whirlwind tour of one of the most powerful, yet easy-to-use, electronic spreadsheet packages—Microsoft Excel 4.0. One goal of this tour was to introduce you to Excel, and show you most of its major tools and features. That goal is now complete.

So far, you have seen that Excel can be used to create and customize worksheets, to build and manage databases, and to generate colorful, professional charts, graphs, and slide shows.

Excel also has many other tools and features to help you with your calculation tasks. A list of these other features follows:

- A total of nine toolbars with over 130 special tools that you can click and use immediately
- Macro features that let you automate worksheet calculations and procedures
- Worksheet customizing tools, including features that let you build your own custom toolbars
- A spelling checker that checks the spelling of all worksheet text entries
- Statistical and engineering analysis tools
- A database consolidation feature that allows you to easily aggregate information from different worksheets into a separate single worksheet, or into a simple report
- What-if analytical tools that help you manage and organize worksheet calculations and the results of those calculations
- Excel's on-line Help features and Product Support services

Now that your initial tour is complete, we suggest that you acquire a version of Excel, and begin your own product explorations. To start, try out Excel's helpful on-line tutorials, and read through the product's documentation.

But, most importantly, begin building worksheets that help you with your home, school, and office calculation tasks. As you do so, when you need the power of a modern, electronic spreadsheet, you will simply call upon Excel.

$5\sqrt{\Sigma}$
$20 =$

Installing Excel on Your Computer

A

Excel is available in two versions, one for PC-compatible computers that operate in the Windows environment, and another for Macintosh computers.

Microsoft Excel for Windows runs under Windows on a PC-compatible computer with at least 2 megabytes of random-access memory (RAM) and a hard-disk drive.

Microsoft Excel for the Macintosh runs on a Macintosh with at least 1 megabyte of random-access memory (RAM) and a hard-disk drive. More RAM is required if you are using MultiFinder or system software version 7.0 or later.

Excel provides the following setup options:

- *Complete setup* This setup installs Excel and nearly all of the optional files on the several disks contained in the Excel package. For Excel 4.0, this setup option requires about 11 megabytes of hard-disk space. This setup is very simple and is recommended for novices.

- *Minimum setup* This setup option installs only the files you need to run Excel. It doesn't install optional file groups such as the on-line tutorial. For Excel 4.0, this option requires 5 megabytes of hard-disk space.

- *Custom setup* This setup choice installs the necessary Excel files, and then allows you to choose which optional files you wish to install.

- *Network setup* For information on installing Excel on a network, refer to the *Microsoft Excel User's Guide 1* that is packaged with Excel. You can also read the NETWORK.TXT file on the Setup disk for Windows, or the README--NETWORK file on the Setup disk for the Macintosh.

Excel for Windows

To install Excel for Windows, follow these steps:

1. Start your computer in Windows.

2. Access the Program Manager or the File Manager.
3. Insert the Excel disk labeled "Setup" into disk drive A.
4. From the File menu, choose Run. You will see the Run dialog box.
5. In the Run dialog box, type **a:setup**
6. Press the ENTER key or click OK.
7. The Setup program will tell you what to do; just follow the directions on the screen. Answer questions and insert disks as requested. Unless you have a reason to do otherwise, accept Setup's suggestion for the directory name and choose the Complete Installation setup.

Excel for the Macintosh

To Install Excel for the Macintosh, follow these steps:

1. Start your Macintosh.
2. Insert the Excel disk labeled "Setup" in the floppy-disk drive.
3. Double-click the Microsoft Excel Setup icon.
4. The Setup program will tell you what to do; just follow the directions on the screen. Answer questions and insert disks as requested. Unless you have a reason to do otherwise, accept Setup's suggestion for the folder name and choose the Complete Installation setup.

You can cancel the Setup procedure at any time. If you do so, Setup will return your computer to the state it was in before you ran the Setup program.

After installing Excel, browse through the README files for information about various Excel topics. In Excel for Windows, choose any README icon in Excel's Program Manager group. On the Macintosh, double-click any of the README files in Excel's folder.

Toolbars: Click Access to Tools

Excel provides a large selection of tools. You can access Excel's tools by using menus or toolbars. When you start Excel, you see the menu bar and the standard toolbar.

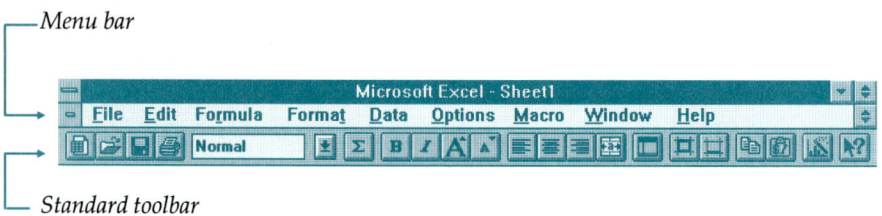

Menu bar and standard toolbar

The Standard Toolbar

The standard toolbar gives you click access to 21 frequently used tools. Simply click an icon to choose the tool the icon represents. You can also gain access to these tools by using menu options. Choose the appropriate menu (File, Edit, Formula, and so on), and then choose a tool from the choices in the menu. Table B-1 briefly describes the tools on the standard toolbar and shows, if available, the corresponding selections you make to access the tool from a menu.

Tool	Menu	Command	Use the Tool to Do This
	File	New	Create a new worksheet
	File	Open	Display the Open dialog box. Use to open an existing document
	File	Save	Save the active document

Appendix B: Toolbars: Click Access to Tools

Tool	Menu	Command	Use the Tool to Do This
🖨	File	Print	Print the active document using the current page setup and printer settings
Normal	Format	Style	Choose a style for a selected range of cells
Σ	Formula	Paste Function	Paste the SUM function and a proposed range into the active cell
B	Format	Font	Make selected information appear bold
I	Format	Font	Make selected information appear italic
A▲	Format	Font	Increase the font size of selected information to the next largest font size
A▼	Format	Font	Decrease the font size of selected information to the next smallest font size
≣	Format	Alignment	Align selected information to the left
≡	Format	Alignment	Center selected information
≣	Format	Alignment	Align selected information to the right
↔	Format	Alignment	Center text from one cell horizontally across selected columns

Tool	Menu	Command	Use the Tool to Do This
	Format	AutoFormat	Apply a previously chosen AutoFormat to selected information
	Format	Border	Add a border around a selected range of cells
	Format	Border	Add or delete a border along the bottom edge of selected cells
	Edit	Copy	Copy selected information to the Clipboard
			Paste to selected cells only the formats from information that has been copied to the Clipboard
			Start the ChartWizard, which assists you in creating or editing a chart
			Changes the mouse pointer to a question mark. Clicking a screen region or choosing a tool then displays information about your choice. Click this tool again to remove the question mark. Double-click it to get the Help system's Search dialog box

Excel's Other Toolbars

The standard toolbar gives you quick access to 21 frequently used tools. It is one of nine Excel toolbars:

Standard
Formatting
Utility
Chart
Drawing
Microsoft Excel 3.0
Macro
Stop Recording
Macro Pause

Together, these nine toolbars provide access to more than 130 tools. Some tools appear on more than one toolbar. You can display any of the nine toolbars by pulling down the Options menu and choosing the Toolbars command.

Toolbars command on the Options menu

The Toolbars dialog box lists the nine available toolbars. You can use this dialog box to hide a visible toolbar or to show a hidden toolbar.

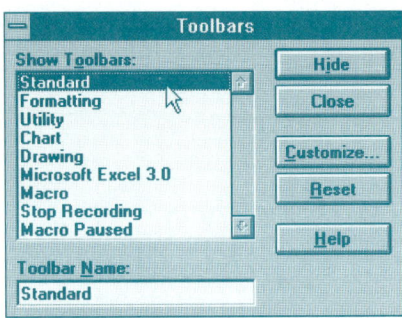

Toolbars dialog box

You can click the Hide button to hide it. To show a hidden toolbar, highlight its name; the Hide button becomes the Show button. Click the Show button to display the highlighted toolbar.

Excel even lets you build your own toolbars. You can build custom toolbars that contain the tools you want, in combinations that suit your style.

For more information about Excel's toolbars, read Chapter 4, "Customizing Microsoft Excel" in *User's Guide 2*, one of the manuals in the Excel package. The *User's Guide* shows the tools on the nine toolbars and a few additional tools that you can add to an existing toolbar, or to your custom toolbars.

The Excel 4.0 Environment

C

This appendix lists some of the specifications of the Excel 4.0 environment. For a more detailed list, refer to the Appendix in the *Microsoft Excel User's Guide 2*.

Tools and Toolbars

Excel provides nine built-in toolbars with a total of more than 130 tools. The names of the toolbars are Standard, Formatting, Utility, Chart, Drawing, Microsoft Excel 3.0, Macro, Stop Recording, and Macro Pause. You can also construct your own custom tools and toolbars.

See Appendix B of this book and the *Microsoft Excel User's Guide 1* for information on using tools and toolbars. See *Microsoft Excel User's Guide 2* for information on creating your own custom tools and toolbars.

Worksheets and Macro Sheets

Here are Excel 4.0's specifications for worksheets and macro sheets:

Maximum sheet size	16,384 rows by 256 columns
Column width	0 to 255 characters
Row height	0 to 409 points (1 point = 1/72 inch)
Maximum length of a formula	1,024 characters
Number precision	15 digits
Number range (exponential notation)	1E-307 to about 1E308
Maximum number of colors per sheet	16

Database Specifications

Excel databases have the following maximum limits:

Maximum number of records	16,383
Maximum number of fields (in one record)	256
Maximum length of a field (characters)	256

Charts

Excel chart documents have the following limits:

Maximum number of data points in one series	4,000
Maximum number of data series in one chart	255
Maximum number of data points in one chart	32,000

File Formats and Filenames

If you are a Macintosh user, you should name files as you would name any other file for the Macintosh. You might want to include information in the filename that tells you the type of file (worksheet, chart, database, and so on). Filenames can be up to 31 characters in length.

If you are a Windows user, Excel 4.0 for Windows automatically attaches filename extensions that indicate the type of file. Normal Excel file formats and filename extensions are listed here. The part of a filename that precedes the filename extension can be up to eight characters in length.

Type of File	Filename Extension	Example
Worksheet	.XLS	CREDCARD.XLS
Chart	.XLC	CREDCARD.XLC
Macro sheet	.XLM	SWAPROWS.XLM
Workbook	.XLW	MILEAGE.XLW
Add-in macros	.XLA	ALGEBRA.XLA
Template	.XLT	UTILBILL.XLT

Excel also has file formats that you can use to export files to other applications or to import files from other applications.

Type of File	Filename Extension
Text for Windows, Macintosh, or DOS	.TXT
Symbolic link format (Multiplan)	.SLK
Comma-separated values format (commas between cell values)	.CSV
Lotus 1-2-3 for Windows	.WK3, .FM3
dBASE IV	.DBF 4

Function Junction

D

Excel can perform many tasks by using only the simple arithmetic operations found on an inexpensive solar-powered calculator: addition, subtraction, multiplication, and division. For more complex applications, you can call on Excel's rich repertoire of built-in *functions*. Excel provides more than 700 functions. For detailed information on Excel functions, consult the *Function Reference* manual that is packaged with the product.

Excel has two types of functions, *worksheet functions* and *macro functions*. You can use macro functions in macro sheets to automate things you might otherwise do manually, such as selecting data, choosing tools, and making choices in dialog boxes. This appendix provides a brief introduction to worksheet functions only. To get information about the over 400 macro functions, look at the *Microsoft Excel Function Reference*.

Worksheet Functions

You can use worksheet functions anywhere within Excel. The simplest type of worksheet function operates on one value, called the *argument of the function*, and produces one result, called the *value of the function*. An example is the square root function. The Excel name for this function is SQRT. It works much like the square root key on a pocket calculator. Here are two examples using Excel's SQRT function.

Example	Argument	Value of Function
SQRT(16)	16	4
SQRT(B5)	The number in cell B5	Square root of the number in B5

Some functions can operate on two or more arguments to produce a value. An example is the COMBIN function. It calculates the number of ways you can select a number of objects from an equal or larger number of objects. For example, you can use the COMBIN function to compute the number of ways to select a set of numbers in a lottery. The following examples use COMBIN to calculate the number of ways to select a set of six numbers from a set of 49 numbers (6 out of 49 lottery) and the number of ways to select a set of seven numbers from a set of 53 numbers (7 out of 53 lottery).

Appendix D: Function Junction

Example	Arguments	Value of Function
COMBIN(49,6)	49 and 6	13983816
COMBIN(53,7)	53 and 7	154143080

If you buy one set of six numbers for the 6 out of 49 lottery, your chance of winning is one in 13,983,816. For the 7 out of 53 lottery, your chance of winning is one in 154,143,080. Good luck!

Many Excel functions can operate on an entire range of data. For example, you can use the SUM function to compute the sum of a range of numbers. The SUM function is used so frequently that it is on the standard toolbar. Its icon is the Greek letter sigma (Σ). The following examples show three ways to calculate the sum of the numbers in cells A1, A2, A3, A4, and A5.

Example	Arguments
=A1+A2+A3+A4+A5	The numbers in cells A1, A2, A3, A4, and A5
=SUM(A1,A2,A3,A4,A5)	The numbers in cells A1, A2, A3, A4, and A5
=SUM(A1:A5)	The range A1:A5 (the numbers in cells A1 through A5)

You can most easily use the SUM function by first selecting the cell where you want the function to appear, and then clicking the SUM icon on the standard toolbar. The SUM function and a proposed range will appear in the formula bar. You can then accept the suggested range, or change it. In the sheet shown here, you can use this method to calculate the student averages and the quiz averages.

	A	B	C	D	E
1					Student
2	Student	Quiz 1	Quiz 2	Quiz 3	average
3	Aloysious Anonymous	73	74	78	
4	Charlemagne Brown	77	82	83	
5	Philistina Shlafly	81	76	66	
6	Bartholomew Simpson	63	58	60	
7	Mariko vos Savant	100	99	100	
8	Quiz average	79	78	77	
9					

Worksheet to calculate quiz averages

First, calculate the student averages in cells E3 through E7. Make E3 the active cell (click E3). Then click the SUM icon in the standard toolbar. You will see the SUM function and a proposed range in the formula bar, as follows:

=SUM(B3:D3)

Excel has cleverly guessed that you want the sum of the numbers in cells B3, C3, and D3. That range is correct, so complete the formula to calculate the average, as shown here:

=SUM(B3:D3)/3

Click the enter box (√) or press ENTER to install the formula in E3. Then, using the fill handle, click and drag cell E3 to cell E7 to get the rest of the student averages.

To calculate the quiz averages, make B8 the active cell, and then click the SUM icon on the standard toolbar. You will see the following in the formula bar:

=SUM(B3:B7)

Excel proposes the range B3:B7. That's the correct range, so complete the formula as follows:

=SUM(B3:B7)/5

Click the enter box (√) or press ENTER to install the formula in B8. Using the fill handle, click and drag cell B8 to cell D8 to install the quiz average formulas. This completes the worksheet. In the illustration, note that formatting tools have been used to show the averages rounded to the nearest whole number.

	A	B	C	D	E
1					Student
2	Student	Quiz 1	Quiz 2	Quiz 3	average
3	Aloysious Anonymous	73	74	78	75
4	Charlemagne Brown	77	82	83	81
5	Philistina Shlafly	81	76	66	74
6	Bartholomew Simpson	63	58	60	60
7	Mariko vos Savant	100	99	100	100
8	Quiz average	79	78	77	
9					

Worksheet with formulas in place

Appendix D: Function Junction   **187**

The Paste Function Feature

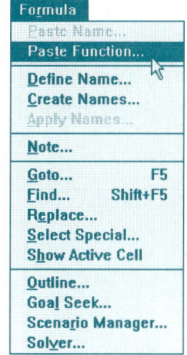

Paste Function command on the Formula menu

Excel has more than 300 worksheet functions. Fortunately, you don't have to memorize their names. When you need a function, you can pull down the Formula menu and choose the Paste Function command.

You then see the Paste Function dialog box, which has a list of functions arranged alphabetically within categories.

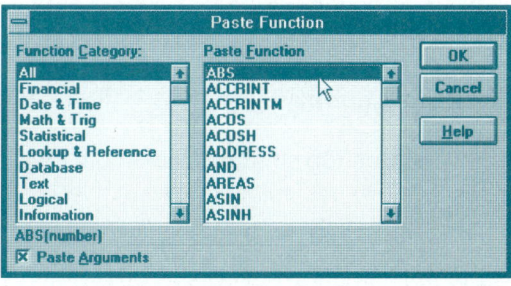

Paste Function dialog box

Use the Paste Function feature to compute the student averages and quiz averages in the worksheet shown previously. Here is the worksheet again in its original state, without the desired student averages.

	A	B	C	D	E
1					Student
2	Student	Quiz 1	Quiz 2	Quiz 3	average
3	Aloysious Anonymous	73	74	78	
4	Charlemagne Brown	77	82	83	
5	Philistina Shlafly	81	76	66	
6	Bartholomew Simpson	63	58	60	
7	Mariko vos Savant	100	99	100	
8	Quiz average	79	78	77	
9					
10					

Worksheet to calculate quiz averages

Compute the student averages. Select cell E3, pull down the Formula menu, and choose the Paste Function command. The Paste Function dialog box appears. In the Function Category list box, choose Statistical. You should see a list of statistical functions in the Paste Function list box. The second function from the top is AVERAGE.

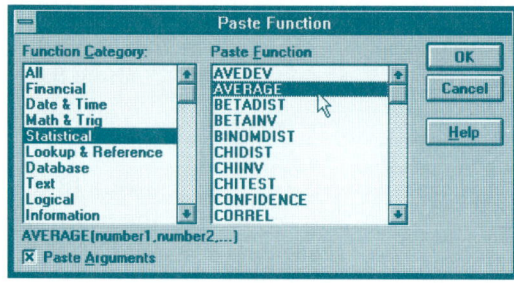

Paste Function dialog box

Highlight the AVERAGE function and click the OK button to choose it and dismiss the Paste Function dialog box. You should now see the following in the Formula bar:

=AVERAGE(number1,number2,...)

Edit the AVERAGE function so that it looks like this:

=AVERAGE(B3:D3)

When the AVERAGE function appears as just shown, click the enter box (√) or press ENTER to install it in cell E3. You can then copy the formula to cells E4, E5, E6, E7.

Now select cell B8 and again use the Paste Function feature to put the AVERAGE function in the formula bar. It looks like this:

=AVERAGE(number1,number2,...)

Note that number1 is highlighted. Click cell B3 and number1 will be replaced by B3, as shown here:

=AVERAGE(B3,number2,...)

Appendix D: Function Junction **189**

Double-click number2 in order to select and highlight it. Then click cell B7. Excel replaces number2 with B7 and the AVERAGE function now looks like this:

=AVERAGE(B3,B7,...)

You are almost finished. Replace the first comma with a colon; then delete the second comma and the three periods so that the function looks like this:

=AVERAGE(B3:B7)

Click the enter box (√) or press ENTER to install the function in cell B8; then copy it to cells C8 and D8. This completes the worksheet.

Names of Worksheet Functions

Excel's worksheet and macro functions are organized by the categories shown next. You can see these categories in the Paste Function dialog box. One way to get detailed information on functions is to highlight the name of the function in the Paste Function dialog box, and then click the Help button. Another way is to consult the *Microsoft Excel Function Reference* that comes with the Excel product. It contains detailed descriptions of all Excel functions.

Function Categories
Financial
Date & Time
Math & Trig
Statistical
Lookup & Reference
Database
Text
Logical
Information
DDE/External
Engineering

The names of all worksheet functions are shown here, within categories. Many function names are reasonably self-descriptive to people who are knowledgeable about the category.

Financial Functions

ACCRINT	ACCRINTM	COUPDAYSBS	COUPDAYS
COUPDAYSNC	COUPNCD	COUPNUM	COUPPCD
CUMIPMT	CUMPRINC	DB	DDB
DISC	DOLLARDE	DOLLARFR	DURATION
EFFECT	FV	FVSCHEDULE	INTRATE
IPMT	IRR	MDURATION	MIRR
NOMINAL	NPER	NPV	ODDFPRICE
ODDFYIELD	ODDLPRICE	ODDLYIELD	PMT
PPMT	PRICE	PRICEDISC	PRICEMAT
PV	RATE	RECEIVED	SLN
SYD	TBILLEQ	TBILLPRICE	TBILLYIELD
VDB	XIRR	XNPV	YIELD
YIELDDISC	YIELDMAT		

Date & Time Functions

DATE	DATEVALUE	DAY	DAYS360
EDATE	EOMONTH	HOUR	MINUTE
MONTH	NETWORK-DAYS	NOW	SECOND
TIME	TIMEVALUE	TODAY	WEEKDAY
WORKDAY	YEAR	YEARFRAC	

Math & Trig Functions

ABS	ACOS	ACOSH	ASIN
ASINH	ATAN	ATAN2	ATANH
BASE	CEILING	COMBIN	COS

COSH	EVEN	EXP	FACT
FACTDOUBLE	FLOOR	GCD	INT
LCM	LN	LOG	LOG10
MDETERM	MINVERSE	MMULT	MOD
MROUND	MULTINO-MIAL	ODD	PI
PRODUCT	QUOTIENT	RAND	RAND-BETWEEN
ROUND	SERIESSUM	SIGN	SIN
SINH	SQRT	SQRTPI	SUM
SUMPRODUCT	SUMSQ	SUMX2MY2	SUMX2PY2
SUMXMY2	TAN	TANH	TRUNC

Statistical Functions

AVEDEV	AVERAGE	BETADIST	BETAINV
BINOMDIST	CHIDIST	CHIINV	CHITEST
CONFIDENCE	CORREL	COUNT	COUNTA
COVAR	CRITBINOM	DEVSQ	EXPONDIST
FDIST	FINV	FISHER	FISHERINV
FORECAST	FREQUENCY	FTEST	GAMMADIST
GAMMAINV	GAMMALN	GEOMEAN	GROWTH
HARMEAN	HYPGEODIST	INTERCEPT	KURT
LARGE	LINEST	LOGEST	LOGINV
LOGNORM-DIST	MAX	MEDIAN	MIN
MODE	NEGBINOM-DIST	NORMDIST	NORMINV
NORMSDIST	NORMSINV	PEARSON	PERCENTILE
PERCENT-RANK	PERMUT	POISSON	PROB
QUARTILE	RANK	RSQ	SKEW

SLOPE	SMALL	STANDARDIZE	STDEV
STDEVP	STEYX	TDIST	TINV
TREND	TRIMMEAN	TTEST	VAR
VARP	WEIBULL	ZTEST	

Lookup & Reference Functions

ADDRESS	AREAS	CHOOSE	COLUMN
COLUMNS	FASTMATCH	HLOOKUP	INDEX
INDIRECT	LOOKUP	MATCH	OFFSET
ROW	ROWS	TRANSPOSE	VLOOKUP

Database Functions

CROSSTAB	DAVERAGE	DCOUNT	DCOUNTA
DGET	DMAX	DMIN	DPRODUCT
DSTDEV	DSTDEVP	DSUM	DVAR
DVARP			

Text Functions

CHAR	CLEAN	CODE	DOLLAR
EXACT	FIND	FIXED	LEFT
LEN	LOWER	MID	PROPER
REPLACE	REPT	RIGHT	SEARCH
SUBSTITUTE	T	TEXT	TRIM
UPPER	VALUE		

Logical Functions

| AND | FALSE | IF | NOT |
| OR | TRUE | | |

Information Functions

CELL	ERROR.TYPE	INFO	ISBLANK
ISERR	ISERROR	ISEVEN	ISLOGICAL
ISNA	ISNOTEXT	ISNUMBER	ISODD
ISREF	ISTEXT	N	NA
TYPE			

DDE/External Functions

CALL

Engineering Functions

BESSELI	BESSELJ	BESSELK	BESSELY
BIN2DEC	BIN2HEX	BIN2OCT	COMPLEX
CONVERT	DEC2BIN	DEC2HEX	DEC2OCT
DEGREES	DELTA	ERF	ERFC
GESTEP	HEX2BIN	HEX2DEC	HEX2OCT
IMABS	IMAGINARY	IMARGUMENT	IMCONJUGATE
IMCOS	IMDIV	IMEXP	IMLN
IMLOG10	IMLOG2	IMPOWER	IMPRODUCT
IMREAL	IMSIN	IMSQRT	IMSUB
IMSUM	OCT2BIN	OCT2DEC	OCT2HEX
RADIANS	SQRTPI		

Reading About Excel

The Excel package contains several books that, taken together, provide a comprehensive reference guide to Excel.

- *Microsoft Excel User's Guide 1* is the primary reference book for most Excel features. It includes information on worksheet, chart, and database features.
- *Microsoft Excel User's Guide 2* provides information on data analysis, custom worksheet functions, and customizing Excel.
- *Microsoft Excel Function Reference* is a comprehensive guide to worksheet and macro functions.

Alternative reference guides are available from several publishers. Visit your local bookstores and computer stores to find one that you like. We suggest the following book for Windows users.

- *Excel 4 for Windows: The Complete Reference* by Martin S. Matthews and Stephanie Seymour, Osborne McGraw-Hill, Berkeley, CA 1993.

There are also many tutorial books designed to help beginners begin using Excel. Try one of the following:

- *Excel 4 for Windows Made Easy* by Martin S. Matthews, Osborne McGraw-Hill, Berkeley, CA 1992.
- *Microsoft Excel Step by Step, 2nd Edition* by Microsoft Corporation, Microsoft Press, Redmond, WA 1992. Available in both Windows and Macintosh editions.

Excel is a power tool for teachers and students. For ideas on using Excel in education, try the following column in *The Computing Teacher, Journal of the International Society for Technology in Education* (ISTE).

- "Power Tools for Math and Science," *The Computing Teacher* by Bob Albrecht and George Firedrake, ISTE, 1787 Agate Street, Eugene, OR 97403-1923.

Index

#DIV/0!, error message, 132
$, absolute cell reference, 35
<, less than symbol, search criterion, 68
<=, less than or equal to symbol, search criterion, 68
<>, not equal to symbol, search criterion, 68
=, equal symbol, search criterion, 68
=, to indicate a formula, 12, 133
>, greater than symbol, search criterion, 68
>=, greater than or equal to symbol, search criterion, 68
[Book1]MILEAGE.XLS!$D$1, 151
1974 RX4 Mileage Data chart, 140
1974 RX4 Mileage Data worksheet, 130
1st key, Sort dialog box, 69
2nd key, Sort dialog box, 69
3-D column chart, 52, 103
3-D line chart, 52
3-D pie chart, 51, 53
3-D View command, Format menu, 107
3rd key, Sort dialog box, 69

A

Absolute cell reference, 35
Active cell, 9
Add to Workbook dialog box, 146
Adding a database record, 74

197

Adding text to a chart, 53
Align center icon, Standard toolbar, 171
Align left icon, Standard toolbar, 171
Align right icon, Standard toolbar, 171
Ants, marching, 44
Apple Macintosh, 2, 18
Area chart, 49
    3-D, 51
    tool, 49
Argument, of a function, 184
Arrow, dragging it, 55
Arrow tool, 55
AutoFormat icon, Standard toolbar, 171
AVERAGE function, 188

B

Bold Font icon, Standard toolbar, 27, 171
Boldface font, 25
Books about Excel, 196
Border command, Format menu, 30
Border icon, Standard toolbar, 171
Bound document, 147
Bound note, 160
Browsing a database, 64

C

Case insensitive search, 65
Category (X) Axis Labels, ChartWizard, 139
Category list box, Number Format dialog box, 29
Cell, 9
    active, 9
    text box, 157
    worksheet, 9
Cell Note dialog box, 157
Cell reference, absolute, 35
Cell reference, relative, 35

Center across columns icon, Standard toolbar, 171
Changing column width, 32
Chart, 4, 42, 102
    1974 RX4 Mileage Data, 140
    3-D area, 51
    3-D column, 52, 103
    3-D line, 52
    3-D pie, 51, 53
    adding text, 53
    area, 49
    column, 107
    custom note, 54
    deleting a, 143
    editing a, 104, 107
    Estimated Multimedia Revenues, 47
    expanding to a window, 103
    filename extension (XLC), 142
    imbedded, 141
    legend tool, 51
    line, 137
    link to worksheet, 149
    MPG.XLC, 143, 153
    object, 104
    pie, 50
    removing a legend, 139
    rotating a, 105
    selecting an object, 111
    selection handles, 104, 105, 108
    specifications, 179
    stacked column, 49
    toolbar, 48
    wireframe image, 105, 109
Chart title, ChartWizard, 140
Chart tool, area, 49
Chart toolbar, 48
    arrow tool, 55
    legend tool, 51

text tool, 53
ChartWizard, 43, 102
    dialog box, 44, 136
    legend, 46
    titles, 47
    X-axis labels, 46
    X-axis title, 140
    Y-axis title, 140
ChartWizard icon, Standard toolbar, 171
Check mark icon, Formula bar, 86
Clear command, Edit menu, 81
Clearing a column, 81
Click and drag, 26
    fill handle, 93, 134
Clipboard, copying graphics to, 118
Clipboard, pasting graphics from, 119
Close Workbook command, File menu, 153
Column, 9
    clearing a, 81
    deleting a, 82
    highlighting a, 82
    inserting a, 84
    selecting a, 82
Column chart, 107
    3-D, 52, 103
Column Width command, Format menu, 32
COMBIN function, 184
Command key, 111
    nonadjacent cell selection, 136
Computing Teacher, 196
Constant, 10
    numeric, 22
    value, 10
Copy, Standard toolbar, 170
Copy command, Edit menu, 34, 118
Copy icon, Standard toolbar, 170
Copying a formula, 34

Copying graphics to the Clipboard, 118
Country & Western database, 58, 156
Country & Western worksheet, 60
Credit Card Procrastination worksheet, 30, 80
CSV, filename extension, 180
CTRL key, 111
    nonadjacent cell selection, 136
CTRL-ENTER, to insert blank line, 157
Currency, number format, 39
Custom note, chart, 54

D

DANCEDAT.XLS, database form, 63
Data menu, 62
    Form command, 63, 74
    Series command, 97
    Set Database command, 62
    Sort command, 69
Database, 4, 58
    adding a record, 74
    browsing it, 64
    Country & Western, 58, 156
    field, 60
    functions, list of, 192
    range, 61
    record, 61
    search criteria, 65
    specifications, 178
    sort feature, 68
Date, number format, 39
Date & Time Functions, list of, 190
Day-month (dd-mmm) format, 131
DBF 4, filename extension, 180
DDE/External functions, list of, 193
Decrease font size icon, Standard toolbar, 171
DEL key, to delete a chart, 143
Delete command, Edit menu, 84

Deleting a chart, 143
Deleting a column, 82
Dialog box, 25
    Add to Workbook, 146
    Cell Note, 157
    ChartWizard, 44, 136
    Edit Slide Show, 122-123
    Font, 25
    Form, 63
    New, 121, 144
    Number Format, 29
    Paste Function, 187
    Paste Function command, 187
    Save As, 30, 141
    Select Special, 88
    Series, 97
    Sort, 69
    Start Show, 125
    Toolbars, 112, 174
Division by zero error message, (#DIV/0!), 132
Document, 147
    [Book1]MILEAGE.XLS!$D$1, 151
    bound, 147
    unbound, 147
Dollar sign ($), absolute cell reference, 35
Dragging, 44
    a text box, 54
    an arrow, 55
    the fill handle, 93, 134
    with mouse, 44
Drawing toolbar, 112
Drawing tools, 112
    list of, 113

E

Edit menu, 34
    Clear command, 81

Copy command, 34, 118
Delete command, 81
Fill Down command, 94
Fill Right command, 94
Insert command, 84
Insert Paste command, 86
Paste command, 34, 119
Undo Delete command, 83
Undo Sort command, 70
Edit Slide Show dialog box, 122-123
Editing charts, 104, 107
Editing graphic objects, 120
Engineering functions, list of, 193
Enter box, Formula bar, 86
Equal sign (=), to indicate a formula, 12, 133
Error message, division by zero (#DIV/0!), 132
Estimated Multimedia Revenues chart, 47
Estimated Multimedia Revenues worksheet, 42, 47
Excel, 2
    environment, 178
    installing, 166
Excel 4 for Windows: The Complete Reference, 196
Excel 4 for Windows Made Easy, 196

F

Field, database, 60
Field name, database, 60
File formats, 179
File menu, 30
    Close Workbook command, 153
    New command, 121, 144
    Save As command, 141
    Save command, 30, 74
    Save Workbook command, 153
Filename, 142, 179
    extensions, 179
    in Workbook Contents window, 147

CSV extension, 180
DBF 4 extension, 180
FM3 extension, 180
SLK extension, 180
TXT extension, 180
WK3 extension, 180
XLC extension, 142, 179
XLM extension, 142, 179
XLS extension, 142, 179
XLT extension, 142, 179
XLW extension, 142, 179
Fill Down command, Edit menu, 94
Fill, 92
    feature, worksheet, 92
    handle, click and drag, 93, 134
    handle, dragging it, 93, 134
    handle, worksheet, 92, 134
Fill Right command, Edit menu, 94
Financial functions, list of, 190
FM3, filename extension, 180
Font, boldface, 25
Font command, Format menu, 25
Font dialog box, 25
Font size, increasing it, 25
Form command, Data menu, 63, 74
Form dialog box, 63
Format, day-month (dd-mmm), 131
Format menu, 25
    3-D View command, 107
    Border command, 30
    Column Width command, 32
    Font command, 25
    Number command, 29, 141
    Patterns command, 30
Formats, numbers, 29
Formats, files, 179

Formatting, worksheet, 24
Formula, copying it, 34
Formula, worksheet, 23, 33
Formula bar, 7
    check mark icon, 86
    Enter box, 86
Formula menu, 87
    Note command, 157
    Paste Function command, 187
    Select Special command, 87
Function, 184
    argument, 184
    AVERAGE, 188
    COMBIN, 184
    macro, 184
    range, 185
    SQRT, 184
    square root, 184
    SUM, 131, 185
    value, 184
    worksheet, 131, 184
Function Category, Statistical, 188
Function Reference, 184, 196
Functions, 190
    database, list of, 192
    date & time, list of, 190
    DDE/External, list of, 193
    engineering, list of, 193
    financial, list of, 190
    information, list of, 193
    list of, 190
    logical, list of, 192
    lookup & reference, list of, 192
    math & trig, list of, 190
    statistical, list of, 191
    text, list of, 192

G

Graphic objects, editing, 120

H

Help icon, Standard toolbar, 171
Hide button, Toolbars dialog box, 174
Hiding a toolbar, 174
Hiding the Status bar, 60
Highlighting a column, 82
Highlighting a range of cells, 26

I

IBM PC, 2
Icon, 8
Imbedded chart, 141
Increase font size icon, Standard toolbar, 171
Increasing font size, 25
Information functions, list of, 193
Insert command, Edit menu, 84
Insert Paste command, Edit menu, 86
Inserting a blank line, 157
Inserting a column, 84
Installing Excel, Macintosh, 167
Installing Excel, Windows, 166

K

Katy, 58
Key, sort, 69

L

Labels, worksheet, 20
Left Alignment icon, Standard toolbar, 28
Legend, 3.6
    ChartWizard, 3.6
    removing it, 139

Text, ChartWizard, 139
Legend tool, 103
    chart, 51
Line chart, 3-D, 52, 137
Link, chart and worksheet, 149
Logical functions, list of, 192
Lookup & Reference functions, list of, 192
Lottery calculations, 184

M

Macintosh, 2, 18
    setup, 167
Macro, 5
    specifications, 178
Macro, filename extension (XLM), 142
Macro function, 184
Marching ants, 44
Math & Trig functions, list of, 190
Menu bar, 7, 170
Microsoft Excel, 2
Microsoft Excel Function Reference, 184, 196
Microsoft Excel Step by Step, 2nd Edition, 184, 196
Microsoft Excel User's Guide 1, 184, 196
Microsoft Excel User's Guide 2, 184, 196
Microsoft Windows, 2
Mileage data chart, 140
Mileage Data worksheet, 130
MILEAGE.XLS worksheet, 141, 153
MPG.XLC chart, 143, 153
MPGBOOK.XLW workbook, 153
Multimedia Revenues chart, 47
Multimedia Revenues worksheet, 42, 47, 102

N

New command, File menu, 121, 134
New icon, Standard toolbar, 170

New dialog box, 121, 144
Nonadjacent selection of cells, 90, 136
Note, sound, 160
Note, text, 157
Note command, Formula menu, 157
Note indicator symbol, 160
Number command, Format menu, 29, 131
Number format, 29
    Currency, 39
    Date, 39
    dialog box, 29
    Percentage, 39
    Time, 39
Numeric constant, 22

O

Object, chart, 104
One-key sort, 69
Open icon, Standard toolbar, 170
Option-Return, to insert a blank line, 157
Options menu, Toolbars command, 112, 173
Options menu, Workspace command, 60

P

Paste command, Edit menu, 34, 119
Paste Function, 171
    Standard toolbar, 171
    command, Formula menu, 187
    dialog box, 187
    icon, Standard toolbar, 171
Pasting graphics from the Clipboard, 119
Patterns command, Format menu, 30
PC computer, 18
People's Energy Company worksheet, 20
Percentage, number format, 39
Pie chart, 50
    3-D, 53

Power Tools for Math and Science, 196
Presentation tools, 5
Print icon, Standard toolbar, 171

Q

Quiz average worksheet, 185

R

Range, 26
    database, 61
    function, 185
    highlighting a, 26
    selecting a, 26
Record, adding to database, 74
Record, database, 61
Reference functions, list of, 192
Relative cell reference, 35
Rotating a chart, 105
Row, 9

S

Sales Tax worksheet, 10
Save As command, File menu, 141
Save As dialog box, 30, 141
Save command, File menu, 30, 74
Save icon, Standard toolbar, 170
Save Workbook command, File menu, 153
Saving a workbook, 153
Saving a worksheet, 30, 141
Search, case insensitive, 65
Search criteria, database, 65
Search criteria symbols, 68
Select Special command, Formula menu, 87
Select Special dialog box, 88
Selecting a chart object, 26

       a chart object, 111
       a column, 82
       a range of cells, 26
       nonadjacent cells, 90, 136
Selection handles, chart, 104, 105, 108
Series command, Data menu, 97
Series dialog box, 97
Set Database command, Data menu, 62
Setup, Macintosh, 167
Setup, Windows, 166
SHIFT-TAB key, 90
Showing a toolbar, 174
Single key sort, 69
Slide show, 120
       video effects, 123
       worksheet, 122
SLK, filename extension, 180
Sort, 68
       command, Data menu, 69
       dialog box, 69
       feature, database, 68
       key, 69
       one-key, 69
       three-key, 73
       two-key, 72
Sorting a database, 68
Sound note, 160
Spreadsheet, 2, 6
SQRT function, 184
Square root function, 184
Stacked column chart, 49
Standard toolbar, 9, 170
       align center icon, 171
       align left icon, 28, 171
       align right icon, 171
       AutoFormat icon, 172
       bold font, icon, 27, 171

    border icons, 172
    center across columns icon, 171
    ChartWizard icon, 172
    Copy icon, 172
    decrease font size icon, 171
    help icon, 172
    increase font size icon, 171
    New icon, 170
    Open icon, 170
    Paste Function icon, 171
    Print icon, 171
    Save icon, 170
    Style icon, 171
    SUM function, 133, 185
Start Show dialog box, 125
Statistical functions, list of, 191
Status bar, 7
    hiding it, 60
Style icon, Standard toolbar, 171
SUM function, 131, 185
SUM tool, Standard toolbar, 133

T

TAB key, 74, 90
Template, filename extension (XLT), 142
Text, 53
    adding to a chart, 53
    box tool, 53
    dragging it, 54
    functions, list of, 192
    note feature, 157
Three-key sort, 73
Time, number format, 39
Time Functions, list of, 190
Title bar, 7
Titles, ChartWizard, 47
Tool, 53

arrow, 55
drawing, 112
legend, 103
Text box, 53
Toolbar, 7
Chart, 48
Drawing, 112
Standard, 9, 170
Toolbars, 112
command, Options menu, 112, 173
dialog box, 112, 174
list of, 173
Trig functions, list of, 190
Two-key sort, 72
TXT, filename extension, 180

u

Unbound document, 147
Undo Delete command, Edit menu, 83
Undo Sort command, Edit menu, 70
User's Guide 1, 196
User's Guide 2, 196
Utility bill worksheet, 20

v

Value, constant, 10
Value, of a function, 184
Video effects, slide show, 123

w

Width of a column, changing it, 32
Window, Workbook Contents, 145
Windows, 2
Excel setup, 166
Wireframe image, chart, 105, 109
Wizard, chart, 43

Index   213

WK3, filename extension, 180
Workbook, 144
Workbook, filename extension (XLW), 142
Workbook, MPGBOOK.XLW, 153
    saving a, 153
Workbook Contents window, 145
    Bound Document icon, 147
    Chart icon, 147
    filename, 147
    Worksheet icon, 147
Workbook document, [Book1]MILEAGE.XLS!$D$1, 151
Worksheet, 3
    1974 RX4 Mileage Data, 130
    absolute cell reference, 35
    cell, 9
    clearing a column, 81
    column, 9
    Country & Western, 60
    Credit Card Procrastination, 30, 80
    deleting a column, 82
    Estimated Multimedia Revenues, 42, 47
    filename extension (XLS), 142
    fill feature, 92
    fill handle, 92, 134
    formatting, 24
    formula, 23, 33
    function, 131, 184
    functions, list of, 189
    highlighting a column, 82
    imbedded chart, 141
    inserting a column, 84
    labels, 20
    link to chart, 149
    MILEAGE.XLS, 141, 153
    note indicator symbol, 160
    People's Energy Company, 20
    quiz averages, 185

relative cell reference, 35
row, 9
Sales Tax, 10
saving a, 30, 141
selecting a column, 82
slide show, 122
specifications, 178
utility bill, 20
Worksheet icon, Workbook Contents window, 147
Workspace command, Options menu, 60

X

X-axis labels, ChartWizard, 46
X-axis title, ChartWizard, 140
XLA, add-in filename extension, 179
XLC, chart filename extension, 142, 179
XLM, macro filename extension, 142, 179
XLS, worksheet filename extension, 142, 179
XLT, template filename extension, 142, 179
XLW, workbook filename extension, 142, 179

Y

Y-axis title, ChartWizard, 140

The Simply Excel Disk

You can order a disk that contains all the files for the applications shown and described in Simply Excel. This disk also contains many files that are not described in the book. On the Simply Excel Disk, you will find

- Very simple applications designed to help you learn Excel
- The worksheets, charts, databases, and other applications described in the book
- Worksheets that display the formulas used in the applications that appear in the book
- Homework helpers for high school math and science
- Surprises

The Simply Excel Disk has been prepared for your learning enjoyment by the authors with the help of students at the Science School in Santa Rosa, California.

Disks are available in two sizes. Please specify disk size.

_____	5.25" disk $9.95	California residents please add
_____	3.5" disk $9.95	appropriate sales tax.

Disks are shipped first class postpaid. Please allow 2 to 3 weeks for delivery. Send check or money order to:

K & T Enterprises
P.O. Box 1635
Sebastopol, CA 95473-1635

Name: _____

Address: _____

City: _____ State: _____ Zip: _____

Osborne/McGraw-Hill takes NO responsibility for fulfillment of this offer. Specifications subject to change without notice.